# THE SENSE OF RHYTHM

# THE SENSE OF RHYTHM

## A Semiotic Investigation of a Fundamental Device

BY

**GIULIA CERIANI**
*Bergamo University, Italy*

TRANSLATED BY

**SHANNON SANTANGELO**

United Kingdom – North America – Japan – India
Malaysia – China

Il senso del ritmo. Pregnanza e regolazione di un dispositivo fondamentale
by Giulia Ceriani

Emerald Publishing Limited
Emerald Publishing, Floor 5, Northspring, 21-23 Wellington Street, Leeds LS1 4DL

First edition 2024

Original material © Meltemi Editore 2024.
English-language translation © Emerald Publishing published under exclusive licence.
First published as "Il senso del ritmo. Pregnanza e regolazione di un dispositivo fondamentale" by Meltemi Editore.
Translated by Shannon Santangelo.
The moral right of the copyright holder and translator has been asserted.

**Reprints and permissions service**
Contact: www.copyright.com

No part of this book may be reproduced, stored in a retrieval system, transmitted in any form or by any means electronic, mechanical, photocopying, recording or otherwise without either the prior written permission of the publisher or a licence permitting restricted copying issued in the UK by The Copyright Licensing Agency and in the USA by The Copyright Clearance Center. Any opinions expressed in the chapters are those of the authors. Whilst Emerald makes every effort to ensure the quality and accuracy of its content, Emerald makes no representation implied or otherwise, as to the chapters' suitability and application and disclaims any warranties, express or implied, to their use.

**British Library Cataloguing in Publication Data**
A catalogue record for this book is available from the British Library

ISBN: 978-1-83797-031-5 (Print)
ISBN: 978-1-83797-030-8 (Online)
ISBN: 978-1-83797-032-2 (Epub)


Printed and bound by CPI Group (UK) Ltd, Croydon, CR0 4YY

INVESTOR IN PEOPLE

# CONTENTS

| | |
|---|---|
| Introduction to the New Edition | 1 |
| 1. The Rhythmic 'Device' | 5 |
| 2. The Theory of Cultural and Surface Rhythms | 17 |
| 3. The Semiotic Approach | 43 |
| 4. The Rhythmic Gestalt: Constraints and Consequences | 65 |
| 5. The Cognitive Pragmatics of Rhythm | 79 |
| 6. Rhythm as an Aesthetic Tactic | 91 |
| Conclusions | 101 |
| *Bibliography* | *105* |

# INTRODUCTION TO THE NEW EDITION

This book first appeared in 2004. It was for me then the culmination of a research project, in respect of which this publication permitted to establish a provisional standstill, a momentary halt to a long-standing questioning, which saw in the 'rhythm question' one of the most challenging issues in terms of semiotics. And I rightly call it *semiotics*, that is the interface between signifying forms and content matrices, with the added complexity of a morphogenetic anchoring that made it, at the time, a difficult object to handle with a legitimate basis in a rigorously structuralist perspective.

This was, however, my interest in a research at the crossroads of humanities and natural sciences, albeit limited by my lack of that specific scientific area. I would like to express my gratitude to the rigorous guidance of Jean Petitot who invited me to explore those territories as part of my doctoral studies, giving me the courage to do so; of course, I am fully aware that I am the sole responsible for any mistakes I may have made along the way.

The theoretical premise, or at least the underlying question, was (and still is) nevertheless interesting, and all too ambitious: how to justify the 'coercive' nature of a regulatory device which, starting from a system of groupings and repetitions, invests the sensitivity of the perceptive and emotional substratum of the subject of the enunciation, thus producing a double level of discourse? How to do this according to a cogent circularity of extremely high pathemic efficacy, never objectively explained, if not, very partially and only from a linguistic, or literary, point of view – within the analysis of poetic discourse?

And again, how can this be done without surrendering to the overly narrow perspective of discursive rhetoric, cognitive psychology, musicology and embracing instead that interdisciplinary gaze that only semiotics, understood as the principle of order and understanding of a system of signification, allows?

If we have come to a new edition, it is because those questions are still alive today: the answer this book has offered is well-intentioned, albeit partial. We can say we made a decent attempt. But we can equally say that this challenge does not seem to have been particularly taken up by others, for a course of study that would engage in alternative proposals; and my own subsequent research has rather been oriented towards analysis relating to issues that certainly imply a rhythmic process (trends, advertising effectiveness, fashion mechanisms) but – *mea culpa* – without giving sufficient space to insights of a decisively more conceptual matrix with regard to the specific responsibilities of the device itself.

I therefore believe that some of the questions left unanswered by the (non-) conclusions of this book are still open, and deserve to be re-launched through this new edition: in particular, there are at least three thematic tracks on which I would like to bring the debate back to light, following the developments of the last 15 years (both on the front of the semiotic discipline and on that of communication practices):

(1) The theme of the *regulative efficacy* of rhythm, such that we can define it as a 'device' in a privileged way

(2) The theme of *pathemization* resulting from the sensitive recognition of the rhythmic structure

(3) The theme of *transcoding*, i.e. the figural holding of the rhythmic formant, as a guarantee of the inter-textual relationship/conversion.

Nothing too new under the sun, except that, as concerns the first theme, the notion of 'device' has entered into common usage in an extraordinary and widespread way to indicate something else, namely tools concerning technology. What really matters is the shared pragmatic connotation, which stipulates the need for a paced/cadenced (and for this very reason rhythmically groupable) temporal dimension that interrupts the continuous connection flow guaranteed by those same *devices*, and makes it knowable. This is a question I had not yet been raised back in 2004, and which, in my opinion, adds illuminating stimuli when reaffirming the inescapability of rhythmic discontinuity, its systemic relevance, the need for a punctuation of its own to make the flow of digital continuity categorizable (i.e. knowable, graspable).

Of course, this efficacy based on the correspondence between the morphology of the world and the syntax of discourse (as already addressed by Paolo Fabbri, 1991), becomes increasingly complex in its modalization possibilities (theme 2), where morphology is anything but static in the light of digital interfaces – virtual, augmented or 'real' as you like – and the trivialization of discursive categorization that is invested in them is, if anything, more static. But rhythm has a component that cannot be subdued, and much of its charm lies in this provocative nature, and if its syntax becomes repetitive, it drastically loses its symbolic efficacy and its empathetic abilities.

This is the dimension of esthesia, and it is the one with which we deal in theme 3. Driven by the need to find a point of convergence between the different forms of textuality that contemporary society poses to us, it is here that rhythm seems overbearingly relevant, insofar as one wants precisely to consider its figural formant, the deep pattern regulating the exchange between underlying narrative and surfacing figurativeness.

Beyond the urgency posed by these three major thematic strands, it must certainly be emphasized that much has changed on the front of semiotic research in a direction that has made the relatively heretical connotation that this research on rhythm had at the time of its first publication laughable. The interest in substance, in the subject and its perception, brings with it the dimension of what Fontanille (1995) had already called an 'epistemological leap', which is all the more necessary when body language is finally re-actualized by the overall human sciences, in confronting different levels of 'reality' that make universally evident the semiotics of the natural world on which Greimas (1968) had based his own theoretical approach. The alternation that provides moments of conjunction followed by moments of disjunction at the base of the rhythmic group, founds the inter-actantial principle of what will later be inter-subjectivity, introducing an aspectual dynamic to manage the very first level of tense space. In this way, that natural signification of which Greimas had already laid the foundations corresponds to phenomena of discontinuity of a physiological nature (which the body knows in accordance with what is, for example, the flow of circadian rhythms, sucking, breathing, to name but a few) easily read from a semi-symbolic point of view, colored by modulations/figurations of a passionate nature.

But that is not all. If semiotics is more than ready to welcome studies on rhythm that go beyond prosodic normativity, the communication system as a whole has evolved over the last 15 years in a direction we could hardly have imagined, and which in turn puts the question of rhythm back at the core of the matter in a different light. We think, here, of the digital media scenario and the increasing multifunctional nature of the interfaces displayed, and at the same time, of that socialization of communication that emphasizes the phatic and conative functions, in spite of any other implication. Changing the substance of the expression and changing the substance of the content, for forms that primarily aim at involvement on both fronts, thus focus on the management of the relationship, rather than on its quality.

And let us consider, on the other hand, the emergence of artificial intelligence (AI) in our daily lives, which calls for a definite articulation not only of the alternation of contacts but also of content itself according to its know-ability and ability to manage the inter-subjective (and first and foremost inter-actantial) dynamics. If big data is pure flux and continuity, small data is in the hands of those who know how to give plausible figurativeness and tense scope to its potential sense effects. We believe that, in addressing AI-related issues, rhythm can provide the advantage that comes from the unquestionable schematic nature of its binary and periodic proposal, which makes it crucial in the design, and parallel reading, of predictive sequences. However, beyond the formal dimension, what in our opinion is still of greater utility and potential for future development is the unique and physiological matrix of rhythm itself, founded on an alternation of primary Gestalten (tension/distension) ready to be invested narratively in programmes of disjunction/conjunction.

Talking about future research, Greimas wrote as early as in *Dictionnaire* II (1986, p. 191) that it should try to find the presence of a rhythmic Gestalt for the recognition of rhythm as a pregnant form that already comprises a precise content immediately grasped through the semantic universals of knowledge, which are universals of the human mind.[1]

It seems to us that this is precisely the purpose of this research, which attempts to bring the excessively boundless mass of big data back to an identifiable and usable dimension, with the sole aim of establishing a readability that can make the least possible claim to universality.

Here, then, are several, and perhaps not all the reasons for this new edition, which we hope will open up a new front for study, in a more productive way than the first edition did. Compared to the first edition, changes have been slight but hopefully significant: a few minor corrections in language, some bibliographical updates, the deletion of the chapter on natural rhythms, which in my opinion is not sufficiently adapted to the developments made over the years by science in these areas: better then, we believe, to consult the sources directly (see the relevant bibliography, given at least in part below), and stick here to what we can justify in terms of semiotic intelligence.

---

1 *La recherche future devrait essayer de retrouver la présence d'une Gestalt rythmique pour la reconnaissance d'une forme pregnante 'rythme' comportant déjà un contenu précis immédiatement saisi à travers des universaux sémantiques de la connaissance, universaux de l'esprit humain.* A.Greimas, Dictionnaire II (1986, p. 191).

# 1

# THE RHYTHMIC 'DEVICE'

## NOT EVERYTHING IS RHYTHM

*Rhythm* is, on the one hand, the mere recognition of a harmony, external to us as perceivers, and inscribed on the objects of our perception; on the other hand, it is a complex structure that affects our entire system of order and balance.

The dialectic between continuous and discontinuous, on which rhythm *mechanics* is based, is universal. Rhythm is an intimate component of our nature and our deepest inclinations: the search for criteria to recognise and attribute rhythmic structure seeks to establish rhythm as a 'device', a tool of analysis that can account for some of the most delicate intersections between perception and discourse, sensibility and semiotics.

A device is a functional tool, which serves to activate processes and manage interactive mechanisms, no matter whether human or artificial; and it is precisely the redefinition of rhythm as an *active mediator* that interests us.

## FROM THE INEFFABLE TO THE MORPHOLOGICAL

Paul Valery (1973/2000) defines *rhythm* as a difficult notion to analyse, and the usual subdivision of the relations of time seems to him as insufficient, since one is limited to the subsequent and the simultaneous, but between these two there is an intermediate intuition, namely the intuition of rhythm (p. 22).

Paul Valéry is correct when he reproaches the word 'rhythm' for its lack of clarity. But above all, he is right to urge us to adopt a definition that is as simple and transversal as possible; basing it upon the observation of simple phenomena to grasp its intrinsic nature.

In any case, rhythm is certainly not an *ineffable* phenomenon, but rather a *complex morphology*[1] which requires us to consider the congruence of its manifestations.

With this in mind, we set ourselves a twofold objective as of now:

– To avoid any metaphorical use of the rhythmic paradigm in order to always trace it back to the criteria of structure, periodicity and movement.
– To maintain methodological coherence and comparability of results, even for those areas of rhythmic relevance furthest removed from the humanities.

On the other hand, the *fundamental ambivalence* of rhythm had already been emphasised by Claude Lévi-Strauss (1964/1990, p. 16), who established a parallel between music and mythology in his 'Overture' to *The Raw and the Cooked*:

> *We can say that music operates according to two grids. One is physiological – that is, natural: its existence arises from the fact that music exploits organic rhythms and thus gives relevance to phenomena of discontinuity that would otherwise remain latent and submerged, as it were, in time. The other grid is cultural: it consists of a scale of musical sounds, of which the number and the intervals vary from one culture to another.*

Rhythm, in fact, directs the timing of the physiological grid, and induces the aesthetic pleasure of those who experience it through subjection to a double periodicity:

> *[...] that of his respiratory system, which is determined by his individual nature and that of the scale, which is determined by his training. (op.cit., p. 17)*

Many are, therefore, the questions that run through the complexity of the rhythmic phenomenon, culminating in the question that motivates all our research: what is the reason for the evident poignancy of rhythms?

Can it be explained exclusively by a correlation between organic and cultural? And what are the parameters that structure this correlation? And again, are they universal and practically independent of the substance of expression

---

[1] The extensive research carried out by Charles Morazé (1986) shows, in our opinion, the opportunity to conceive of a geometric-topological paradigm, a pre-mathematical form fed by the natural Gestalts selected by our perception and ecological configuration.

and content, or do they change (at least in part) depending on the sphere they 'shape'?

## REPETITION AS PRELIMINARY HYPOTHESIS

Let us therefore assume as a preliminary hypothesis the consideration of rhythm as a structure of repetition.

Repetition can itself be an agent of symmetrical or asymmetrical morphologies, operating on a multiplicity of interval, temporal and spatial dimensions. According to Gilles Deleuze, the repetition of events that characterises a structure of repetition can come in the form of a *repetition-measure* or a *repetition-rhythm*,

> [...] *the first being only the outward appearance or the abstract effect of the second. (1980/1987, p. 21)*

Repetition-measure identifies an isochronous return of identical elements, while repetition-rhythm identifies duration, a succession of irregular intervals. In fact, if /difference/ means the repetition of the non-identical, then rhythm tends more and more toward difference rather than repetition. Along with Félix Guattari, Deleuze further writes on this subject:

> *It is the difference that is rhythmic, not the repetition, which nevertheless produces it. (op.cit., p. 314)*

## RULES AND CONSTRAINTS

*No rhythm*, and consequently, *no constraint*: rules allow not only the recognition, but also the reproduction of a rhythmic structure, regardless of the subject matter of the expression in which it is realised.

*Rhythmic repetition* can be defined as an initially *natural phenomenon*, which then becomes a *semiotic phenomenon* and remains *physically grounded*. It would thus be a peculiar example of 'embodied semiotics' (cf. Varela, Thompson & Rosch, 1991): a form of the natural world that is, at the same time, a form of the constructed world. The notion of emergence, as elaborated by Jean Petitot (1985/2004), will help us in this regard. But let us also formulate the hypothesis – which our work undertakes to confirm or disprove – that rhythm can be equated with a conceptual structure, a mental link between the natural world, the perceived world and the world put into discourse.

## THE PHENOMENOLOGICAL QUESTION OF TIME

It is to Paul Ricœur (1983–1984–1985/1990) that we owe one of the most important observations of the notion of time and its phenomenology: we think it is important and necessary to briefly explore it in order to situate, in parallel, the rhythmic phenomenon.

Ricœur takes up two major 'debates', between Saint Augustine and Aristotle, and between Husserl and Kant, to which he adds a discussion of Heidegger's conception of time. In doing so, he compares cosmological time (the instant) to phenomenological time (the present), and comes to regard this dialectic as the necessary aporia for any speculation on temporality.

For St Augustine in his *Confessions*, the possibility of measuring time resides in the 'distentio animi', i.e. in the extension of the spirit – making abstraction of any external reference to the movements of the Cosmos; Ricœur reproaches Augustine for his failure to replace a *psychological* conception of time with a *cosmological* one.

> *We have only dismissed that the extreme thesis that '"time is constituted by the movement of a material body" [...]. But Aristotle had also refuted it by affirming that, without itself being movement, time was "something of movement".*
>
> *(Ricœur, 1983/1990, p. 15)*

Augustine seeks to find, in expectation and remembrance, some measuring principles independent of the world, and therefore opens the way to absolute relativism.

On the other hand, Aristotle, in *Physics IV*, argues that time 'is not movement, but that by which movement can be numerically estimated' (219b). He postulates that change (i.e. movement) implies time, but that time is also in everything and everywhere, while movement experiences speed and acceleration. Furthermore, according to Aristotle, succession is something to which one is submitted, rather than something imposed as an ordered form on things, since the before and after exist in time well before anteriority and posteriority, according to a logical and narrative sense. When he introduces the notion of 'number' and defines time as 'number of motion in respect of "before" and "after"' (219b1), consciousness is not forgotten here either, as this number must always be measured in difference.

In his critique of these two authors, Ricœur underlines the internal question, not only of time, but also of rhythm, that is, in some way, the 'form' of movement (see Emile Benveniste's fundamental definition of rhythm as the 'form of movement', 1966/1971): an internal conflict in a doubly shared perception, between *objectification* and *subjectification* of a dynamic whose flow surrounds us.

In *On the Phenomenology of the Consciousness of Internal Time* (1928/1991), at the heart of Husserlian conception is the distinction between the phenomena of 'retention' and 'protention', and between retention, which represents primary recollection, and reminiscence, which introduces the notion of secondary recollection.

Retention is in fact an alteration of the original impression, a kind of extended present that is distinct from the duration of the present as such (called *Quellpunkt*):

> ...the consciousness of the now is itself a now, and the consciousness of the enduring presence is itself an enduring presence.
> 
> *(Husserl, 1928/1991, p. 333)*

If Husserlian time is a continuous flux onto which acts of discontinuity are grafted, what interests us about this concept is precisely the *positional* and consequently differential *principle* according to which an event takes its place in time, departing from the present: the *aspectual principle of rhythm as a form* that is overlapped, with its own morphological organisation, to a morphology that is there – but which is external to consciousness, seems to find its foundation here.

After all, according to Paul Ricœur we must deal with the Kantian conception of time and space. In both cases, these are *transcendental* categories, i.e. intuitive and capable of explaining other a priori knowledge. In this sense, time and space seem *invisible* and unknowable, except through the physical determinations that represent them as a drawn line: inner and outer intuition are absolutely parallel, space and time are the two pure forms of sensible intuition.

From this perspective, it is not impossible to imagine the *objective foundation* that Kantian time could bring to any conception of rhythm, freeing it from all relativity and endowing it with the absolute primacy of a *founding scheme*. Paul Ricœur (1985/1990) writes:

> *In one sense, the debate between Husserl and Kant is rendered obsolete – in the same sense that the opposition between subject and object is.*
>
> *(Ricœur, 1985/1990, p. 85)*

In this sense, the Heideggerian consideration of the structure of intra-temporality ('Innerzeitligkeit') through which this author configures his semantics of action, concerns us closely. For Heidegger, in fact, temporality ('Zeitligkeit') is simply the dialectic between being-toward-death, having-been-ness and being-with, which characterises the experience of time. Now, intra-temporality or being-in-time is not reducible to mere cyclical time (Heidegger, 1927/1978).

The phenomenological approach ultimately remains unresolved and non-exhaustive: the path proposed by Jean Petitot to reconcile objectivity and phenomenology, physical modelling and human sciences, in search of those catastrophic infrastructures of phenomena that constitute the *objective correlate* of their perceptual semiotics and linguistic description (Petitot, 1983), points alternatively to an arduous path, but perhaps the only one within which we can put our hypotheses on rhythm to the test of time and space.

## NARRATIVE ISSUES

Throughout Ricœur's theorising, there is a clear-cut stance: the dialectic between time and plot is the essential engine of narrativity, and narrativity itself is first and foremost a way of representing time.

Not opposite, but with profound differences, is the narrative theory of Algirdas J. Greimas, who brings in time at the last moment, when the narrative structures its discourse and when enunciative choices have to be made. Again, as Paul Ricœur (1984/1990, v. II, p. 32) clearly writes:

> *What is at stake in the discussion in narratology concerns, in fact, and in similar manner, the degree of autonomy that should be accorded to the process of logicization and dechronologization in relation to understanding the plot and the time of the plot.*

These two theoretical elaborations, which are not directly concerned with rhythm, but which contain many elements that can help us in our task of definition, do not take into account[2] a third temporal dimension: the one relating to the attending of the story itself. Now, rhythm is certainly involved in the act of interpretation, and this will invite us to take a closer look at the conceptions of time of Gérard Genette and Umberto Eco, who represent this third position.

In the Greimasian approach, the story is the manifestation of the paradigmatic oppositions that ground it in its deep structures. As Patrizia Magli and Maria Pia Pozzato (1985) write, every text is the evidence and memory of its generative history, since it is not simply grasped at the level of its expressive manifestation, but in the way its manifestation is generated and developed in a conversion-oriented process (p. III).

Immediately following the deep level of syntax and fundamental semantics, the narrative level concerns the relations of conjunction and disjunction between subject and object of value. Temporality is, in this case, the architecture that governs narrative programmes, following the orientation of syntactic operations and allowing for the unveiling of relations of *anteriority*, *concurrence* and *posteriority* between programmes.

The spatio-temporal structure then operates as a *neutral grid* that coordinates the conversion process: on this grid, during the elaboration process of discourse, the specific organisation of rhythm is subsequently grafted, the *perceptual poignancy* of which can also be explained, semiotically, by the necessity of this preliminary foundation. For further discussion, we refer to the third chapter of this work, dedicated to the semiotic approach.

We have already discussed Paul Ricœur's position on the phenomenological issues inherent in temporality. What is important to recall here is that for Paul Ricœur, narrative is the human way of conceiving time. The essential criticism he addresses to Algirdas Greimas is that temporality would not be a less profound factor than fundamental semantic relations.

This seems to us a rather minor problem. When Greimas identifies a logical relation in temporality, clearly this is fundamental since, by altering it, the very intelligibility of the narrative would be compromised, and that it is also profound, since it proceeds from the postulation of axiologies and of value systems, to the syntagmatic structure of the logical operations of transformation.

---

2 This is the observation that Daniele Barbieri addresses in his doctoral thesis *Tempo, immagine, ritmo e racconto* [Time, image, rhythm and narrative] (University of Bologna, 1992), dedicated to the semiotics of temporality in comics.

In *Narrative Discourse Revisited* (1983/1988), Gérard Genette distinguishes three different types of temporality: that of the story, that of the narrative and that of narrating. These three levels all exist in relation to the narrative. Their interrelation is categorised according to three categories: *tense, mood* and *voice*; among these, *tense* is in turn subdivided according to determinations of *order, frequency* and *duration*, which refer to the *dispositio* of classical rhetoric. The object of the temporal analysis of narrative is the definition of the relationships between story and discourse: *anachrony, achrony* or *anisochrony*. According to Gérard Genette (op.cit., p. 88), a narrative

> [...] *can do without anachronies, but not without anisochronies, or, if one prefers (as one probably does), effects of rhythm.*

Instead, the notion of the Ideal Reader or Model Reader is at the heart of Eco's approach to the question: a textual strategy designed to 'collaborate' interpretatively, following the same steps that the author has taken generatively. In this way, the text guides the 'inferential strolls' (cf. Eco, 1979) taken by the Model Reader, which are proposed as a privileged path to the empirical receiver, who is free to follow them or develop an autonomous path.

The Model Reader's time is linear in that it concatenates successive points of view, but it is also cumulative in the sense that it produces a kind of memorial synthesis of events that have occurred previously and on which perspectives, forecasts and anticipations can be grafted. This temporality does not necessarily correspond to that of the narration; it also includes the temporality of an 'ideal' reading that can be strongly modalised on the rhythmic level using, for example, the movements of the Model Reader to mimic the dynamics of a real act (see, in this regard, Umberto Eco's post-scriptum to his novel *The Name of the Rose*, where the functioning of rhythmic stylistics to describe an act in rhythmic experience such as an intercourse is clarified); or again, to achieve intensifications or pathemic distensions that correspond, in the act of reading, to the participation of the empirical reader.

The issue of correspondence between syntactic and semantic rhythms, as well as that of the existence and passionate functioning of a *rhythmic style*, is introduced here.

## PLASTIC ISSUES

Rhythm, as we understand it, represents a *recursive* structure – that is, based on repetition but also on the internal solidarity of its constituent elements like a *motif*, which intervenes in the organisation of signification. It is the hypothesis of the existence of *pre-structures of a figural order*, and therefore not yet figurative, which would govern the discursive tensiveness and sub-orchestration of meaning, such as to constitute rhythm as a *phenomenon of style*[3], and as such *plastic* and *Gestalt-like*.

In this sense, rhythm primarily poses the problem of the relationship between perception, sensation and signification and, in this case, that of the *poignancy* of certain semiotic organisations perceptually privileged over others. The question now is whether it is legitimate and appropriate to conceive of a *plasticity of meaning* accordingly, and to understand in what way it would be comparable, in its rhythmic realisation, to a meaningful organisation.

It is certain that, similarly to the spatial perspective, there is a temporal perspective that allows for the programming of textual time starting from the recomposition of individual events (which have their own state of existence) and according to a *setting*, a background that accounts for the coherence of their figures as well as the hierarchy that events establish among themselves. This is certainly a *Gestalt perception* phenomenon, and rhythm assumes an important place within it. Teresa Keane (1991, p. 30) rightly writes, in the process of perception, that the intervention of the subject manifests itself through the projection of a structure that accommodates what is perceived, and which takes the form of an actantial model whose function is to organise the figures of the world.

However, objects involve a class of perceptions that have intrinsic qualities and recognised distinguishing features, which are very much part of our experiential competence and, to quote Teresa Keane again, confirm that there is another dictionary, an encyclopaedic dictionary of the world as imaginary, made up of images glued, embedded or superimposed on each other and constituting our everyday, common-sense reality, coexisting alongside a dictionary of sensations perceived as distinctive traits and formulated as lexemes of natural languages or of an unambiguous language (ibid.).

The encounter between subject and object would thus take place through Gestalten, figures of content in natural language that cross figures of expression in the sensible world to rejoin their discursive manifestation.

---

3 See in this respect no. 9/10, 1993, of the 'Semio-news' journal, particularly the article by Alessandro Zinna, *Teoria narrativa e stilistica* [Narrative theory and stylistics]. This definition is given to us by Jean Petitot, who presented it in his thesis, and by René Thom (1988), who included it in his work *Esquisse d'une sémio-physique* [Outline of a semio-physics], Paris, Interéditions.

The issue raised by Keane is at the heart of our discussion on rhythm: it would serve, as a Gestalt, as a bridge between perception and enunciation, deep figurativeness (which belongs to the sensory world) and semantic figurativeness (which belongs to the subject's linguistic representations; cf. Greimas 1968), to allow, as stated by Pierre Oullet (1992), a good insight into a place that is neither abstract nor concrete, but schematic, in which categorisation is articulated as a processing at the same time of sensory data and verbal representations (p. 4).

The form of expression of any order of discourse would in this sense have a *perceptual correlate* since the figural scheme – and rhythm is one – would translate at the enunciative level the way in which the subject learned and represented for itself the objects of the sensible world. The isomorphism between perceptual and enunciative processes, the homologation of points of view, would explain the poignancy of the rhythmic model at the proprioceptive crossroads between esteroception and interoception.

In conclusion, it could be said that any discourse is capable of representing a situation in a timely manner through its form of expression, but also through the way in which this situation becomes a state of mind and thus an *experience* of both the enunciating and the enunciated subject (cf. Oullet, 1992): through the spatio-temporal coordination of rhythm, one can achieve that *emphasis or perspective*, which allows a *meaningful translation of the sensible*.

As we have already pointed out, this is a *plastic* phenomenon since it influences the structuring of deep figurativeness and functions as an intermediary between manifestation and the fundamental categories, as an interface with the natural world. The schematisation advocated by Jean Petitot to explain emergence phenomena would find an application model here – albeit not yet mathematised.

Here, too, is where the postulation of a *generative path of the plane of expression* could be located. Here, the proposal of a cognitive interface, of a *conceptual structure* based on iconic schemes that structure learning about the world and its processing, could also find a place: an important step towards a non-metaphysical description of the nature of *modal devices*.

## THE RHYTHMIC DEVICE TO THE TEST

Therefore, it is not true that everything is rhythm. It is true however, and this is our hypothesis, that the *rhythmic pattern*, as a bodily pattern, underlies all human activity.

> *We hold with Merleau-Ponty that Western scientific culture requires that we see our bodies both as physical structures and as lived, experiential structures – in short, as both "outer" and "inner", biological and phenomenological. These two sides of embodiment are obviously not opposed.*
>
> *(Varela, Thompson & Rosch, 1991, p. XV)*

In agreement with the authors we have quoted, and according to the great lesson of Maurice Merleau-Ponty, we believe that the body has its own experiential structure and that it is at the same time at the centre of cognitive mechanisms.

In this sense, it is easy to understand the interest we attach to it, far beyond the literary, semiotic and philosophical issues evoked above, and which goes beyond the purely natural and biological question of 'universal' rhythms. The perspective in which we most willingly consider rhythm, and which we will try to justify throughout this study, is in any case twofold, and relates to:

– A form of *emergence*, i.e. complexification of structure linking the organic to the discursive.

– A form of 'embodiment' (cf. Varela, Thompson & Rosch, 1991), or 'embodied action', which shows how perception is in fact a phenomenon driven by the sensorimotor capacities of the body, and how these capacities are in turn rooted in the biological, psychological and cultural layers of human experience.

Rhythm is a form that in itself is neither physical or biological nor semiotic. Rather, it is a *form of phenomenon*, and it is not easy to find a specific position for it, as it actually intervenes in many different phenomena.

For this reason, the path of our research will develop in a highly interdisciplinary manner, following the emergence of rhythms and their transcoding from the natural to the cultural.

# 2

# THE THEORY OF CULTURAL AND SURFACE RHYTHMS

The question of the relation between deep rhythms and the establishment of a subject leads us to introduce the debate on *discursive rhythms or surface rhythms*.

By *surface rhythms*, we mean the rhythmic phenomena concerning speech, whatever the nature of the latter. A more or less pronounced presence of rhythmic intervention can indeed be found in the different types of discourse, verbal and non-verbal, since rhythm as a discursive category is part of the study of the relations between enunciation and utterance, i.e. of every language production.

We will not, however, examine discursive rhythmisation in its individual specificity, but will instead attempt to *account for rhythm as a cognitive Gestalt*, a distinctive form detectable in every discourse *before* its figurative construction. To this end, we will propose a few examples of rhythmisation, which seem most significant to us, in the fields of poetry, music, film and theatre production. These domains explicitly use rhythm as a tactic of representation, and through it seek to manage the emotional and cognitive activity of the spectator, thus testing rhythm's aptitude as a *device*.

In this regard, we would like to point out the importance attributed by a linguist such as Viggo Brøndal to what he called *rhythmicity*. In the 'delimitation and subdivision of grammar', he proposes in his *Essais de linguistique générale* [Essays on general linguistics] (1943, pp. 134–140), Brøndal argues that language has four aspects: it is both system and rhythm, language and word, and the linguistic sign is both internal and external, signified and signifier. In this way, Brøndal succeeds in assimilating rhythmics, i.e. the science of *speech*, to general psychology, thus emphasising the universal and physically motivated side of emotion that invests speech; while syntax studies the internal rhythm of language, prosody studies its external rhythm.

Brøndal (1943, p. 140) affirms that sociology is related to the system side of language, while psychology is related to the rhythm side. Every language has a system that distinguishes that language from all others, whereas the linguistic rhythm is common to all languages.

And it is precisely this very effort to reconcile morphology and intentional dynamics, form and syntax between biology and linguistics that brings us closer to the theoretical conceptions of a rhythmologist such as Claude Zilberberg. Echoing Valéry's suggestion that 'form is time', Zilberberg reinterprets structural thinking according to the essential opposition of the rhythmic group

*concentrated vs. extended*

and concludes with the attribution of rhythm to a virtual level that precedes any expressive realisation, as in the scheme below:

| | | |
|---|---|---|
| RHYTHM | *figural level* | expectation/relaxation |
| | *figurative level* | silence/accent |
| SYSTEM | concentrated/extended | (cf. Zilberberg, 1989). |

In this scheme, what interests us is the idea of envisaging a generative pathway of rhythm that would account for its presence at the level of both the form of expression and that of content, as well as the distinction between a pathemically invested figural level and a figurative level that translates the anterior tension into a discursive setting.

It is from these same assumptions that we will approach the discussion of poetic rhythm.

## POETIC RHYTHM

The question of rhythm in poetry is one of the most pivotal, and of the most debated. The association between poetry and rhythm stands on the threshold of the relationship between rhythm and metre, which are either overlapping or opposing, depending on theoretical approaches. In the first case, as Lucie Bourassa (1990, p. 29) writes, this poetry-rhythm association in opposition to ordinary language often results from a combination of the notion of rhythm with that of metric, where the two systems may agree or oppose each other, while metric always remains the stable element that allows accentual inequality to be perceived. This conception of rhythm has the advantage of not being limited to the phenomena of isometry but always assumes their presence. The different meanings pose a problem when dealing with contemporary texts that make use of types of formal and material arrangements other than those of measured versification: free verse, prose poems, dispersion of segments across the page. Metrics, intended in the strict sense of systematic use of a code of regularities, disappears from a large part of our century's production.

## RHYTHM AND METRE

It is nevertheless clear that the disappearance of metrics did not result in the disappearance of rhythm, and it is therefore possible to justify the hypothesis that rhythm and metre constitute two systems which are not truly opposed, but certainly independent. Therefore, it is not surprising that in its recent re-edition of *Rhétorique de la poésie* [A Rhetoric of Poetry] (1977, p. 150), the Groupe μ insists on an autonomous theory of rhythm that makes a distinction between *protorhythm* and *rhythm* tout court.

As an expression of a cyclical time characterised by the return of any intensive event (phoneme or group of phonemes, syllable or group of syllables, accent, redundant concentration of semes) rhythm would have progressive degrees of existence – where the proto-rhythm consists of two events, the quasi-rhythm of three, while rhythm exists from four events that allow the recognition and reproduction of a temporal law – but would be indifferent to its manifestation within a prose or poetic text stricto sensu, as well as to metrical rules.

In his work on the 'autonomy of the signifier' (L'autonomia del significante, 1975, 83), Gian Luigi Beccaria clearly summarises his thinking in this regard. Referring to the rhythmic figure of alliteration, he says that being constrained by this rhythmic-rhetorical form, the idea marked in this way emerges more intensely, but not because the form has phono-symbolic or even semantic connotations; simply, as an autonomous form, acting outside the consciousness of semanticism, alliteration becomes the sense of words, within and without them, it becomes information, signification. This is precisely the meaning of the autonomy of rhythm.

Rhythm and metre should then be considered as suprasegmental modulations constituting the prosodic level, reproducing the poetic discourse with a skillful play of alternating parallelisms and symmetries (Greimas, 1972, p. 11).

It is in this sense, and on the conviction that the prosodic and syntactic levels are not necessarily isomorphic – the isomorphism would rather lie between the prosodic and semantic levels – that we propose to reconsider the relationship between rhythm and metre from a re-reading of a too often forgotten classic text, *Ritm i sintaksis* [Rhythm and Syntax] by the formalist Osip Brik (1927).

If poetic rhythm is for Brik, a more or less regular alternation in the same way as choreographic or musical rhythm, he nevertheless recognises specificity in it, that of being a movement that precedes quantitative organisation, that is antecedent to verse. One cannot understand rhythm from the line of verse; on the contrary, one will understand verse from the rhythmic movement (O. Brik, in T. Todorov, *Théorie de la Littérature*, 1927, p. 144).

The rhythmic pulse, independent of any quantification of the syllables into tonic, semi-tonic and non-tonic, can theoretically concern any syllabic unit, and thus descends from enunciational competence and not from enunciative performance. As organisation, however, the rhythmic movement distributes intensity and intermittence. Thus, according to Brik, there is a pulse that precedes the iamb and consists of a regular repetition of loud tempos of increasing intensity. In contrast, in the trochaic metre the intensity will be decreasing. All this *pre-exists verbal realisation*. The syllabic materialisation of the rhythmic curve makes the presence of rhythm perceptible and visible, where, however rhythmic units can correspond to much more complex groups and, in a concrete attitude, verse has to be seen as a necessarily linguistic complex regulated by specific laws that do not coincide with those of the spoken language (ibid., p. 153).

However, we think we can measure, if not the rhythm, then at least its range of investment, and that, in this sense, it is still legitimate to distinguish between a *syllabic rhythm* (where time rests on the syllable so that all syllables tend towards an equal duration) and a *rhythm based on the metric foot* (a broader unit that can cover several syllables). The increasing or decreasing pulse makes it possible in both cases to establish a first intonemic distinction between languages.

## RHYTHM AND INTONATION

In M. A. K. Halliday's reflection on the relationship between rhythm and intonation, the foot represents the rhythmic unit of language. It must be differentiated from a higher-ranking constituent element that is the melodic unit of the language, generally referred to as the tonal group, or, more rarely, the 'tonal unit'; melody, as a linguistic trait, is called intonation; the tonal group is thus the higher-ranking intonation unit (1985, p. 9).

According to Halliday, Brik's rhythmic pulse would therefore rather be confused with intonemics, and it is for this reason that he acknowledges its responsibility at the semantic level.

This hypothesis does not convince us, and restricting the question of the rhythmic pulse to orality seems very limiting. We believe we should rather examine rhythmic alliances (not isomorphisms) – the syntactic ones, and also their semantic consequences.

For his part, Roman Jakobson, in his *Principes de versification* [Principles of versification], expresses a completely opposite idea to Halliday's. While it is true that there is a periodicity in expiratory waves, this cannot be approached in the same way as the periodicity that structures poetic rhythm, as poetic time is typically a time of waiting, and at the end of a defined interval we wait for a defined signal (1973, p. 43).

In his view, prosody must distinguish (ibid., p. 52):

(1) The phonological basis of rhythm;

(2) The extra-grammatical accompanying elements;

(3) The autonomous phonological elements, more precisely the phonological elements that are not a factor of rhythmic inertia in the poetic language under consideration.

It is important to understand that rhythmic inertia can be traced in any oral expression; in poetry, marked time can be founded 'on a fact that linguistic consciousness does not distinguish', it can in fact transform the elements of emotional language, anchored in the 'biological matter' that justifies the pathemic rootedness of prosodic energy.

David Bolinger (1970) also took up these concepts and came up with a real 'generative pathway' of intonation, subdivided into four information-controlled layers:

– a grammatical layer (accents, endings, brackets, paragraphs);

– a partially grammatical layer (controlled affective meanings with an informative vocation);

- a non-grammatical layer (non-accented syllables, uncontrolled affective information);
- an originally non-grammatical layer (levels dictated by emotion).

## THE FUNDAMENTAL RHYTHM

Let us return to Brik's work. While the rhythmic pulse is free, to Brik the rhythmic–syntactic configuration is anchored to the verse and its measure, binary or ternary, and this entails combinations of two or three signifying words, i.e. a typical iambic tetrameter, which may be of a varied syntactic nature. He argues that a rhythmic and syntactic word combination differs from a purely syntactic combination because the words are included in a certain rhythmic unit (the verse), and differs from a purely rhythmic combination because the words are combined according to both semantic and phonic qualities (1927, in Todorov, 1985, p. 149).

So, there is, on the one hand, the *fundamental rhythm* of a language, and, on the other hand, the verse that organises its equalities and makes them measurable through the metre. As Zilberberg (1988, p. 154) also points out, while phoneticisation and rhythmisation seem inevitable, metrisation in this sense derives from an eventual, optional order.

Regular verse, as well as verse with variable metre and the verset, have two types of rhythm, that of spontaneous language and that which could be called *metrical rhythm* – the sense effects produced by versification inevitably rests on both.

The first effect is that of the regularity produced by the metre, an immutable reality on which prosodic movement intervenes. Consequently, the canonical form of the verse is given by a few quantified syllabic units that the syncopation of the caesura interrupts by producing a principle of variation. On the side of metric rhythm, we next find rhyme and assonance that allow the verse to strengthen and build up an alternating principle leading to the *fundamental rhythm*: we therefore define prosodic rhythm as a *euphonic system encoded according to a semi-symbolic mode and a perceptually pregnant semantism*. Pause and break, which normally correspond to the demarcation of a sense unit, can introduce a gap between fundamental rhythm and metric rhythm. In addition, as Joseph Pineau (1979, p. 18) writes, any rhythmic analysis requires an examination of

(1) The nature of the rhythmic relays, i.e. in a sound continuum it is necessary to determine whether the rhythmic material is intensity, timbre, pitch, length, etc.;

(2) The quality of strong and weak beats;

(3) Periodicity of the relays, and the quantitative relationship between rhythmic units and, within the same unit, the ratio between momentum and beats;

(4) The eventual hierarchy of beats, i.e. the connections, and the consequent organisation of the rhythmic movement at several levels;

(5) Time and its possible variations;

(6) Finally, the creative principle that transfigures the rhythmic relation and ensures the living unity of the whole.

The rhythmic analysis of a poem is thus very different from its metric analysis, although rhythm is not exempt from a certain quantification that allows variations and intermittences to be *measured* from, for example, the poem's accentual subdivision.

## THE UTOPIA OF A UNIVERSAL RHYTHMICS

One cannot conclude these few notes on poetic rhythm without mentioning the most important, albeit sometimes paradoxical, effort to establish a *universal rhythmics* starting, precisely, from a conception of poetic rhythm that transcends the metre. Think of Henri Meschonnic's *Critique du rythme* [The critique of rhythm] (1982). Polemically, the author writes that in metrics, the alexandrine verse has only two marked positions, the sixth and twelfth, even if in terms of rhythm, the alexandrine has twelve positions (Meschonnic, op.cit., p. 271).

Nevertheless, this definition by Meschonnic, which makes rhythm correspond to the deep identity of the subject, establishing a bridge between deep rhythms and surface rhythms (as well as for us), is completely negative; rhythm, for him, is not metric, but neither is it a form or a structure, as rhythm is the utopia of meaning (ibid., 143).

We will try to demonstrate exactly the opposite, the *non-ineffability* of rhythm and its schematic nature.

In poetics, for example, Pius Servien, in his text *Rythmes comme introduction physique à l'esthétique* (1930) [Rhythms as a physical introduction to aesthetics], speaks of a science of rhythms, and writes that whenever we speak of rhythm, we perceive numbers, in a more or less confused way.

This author proposes a notational method, also applicable to prose, based on representative numbers: the first number, N, has as many digits as tonic accents; its digits indicate how many syllables there are from the tonic one to the next; atonal syllables are indicated by an apostrophe, silences by punctuation or voids. The rhythmic pattern can then be described in its progression and variations by means of an arithmetic number obtained by adding up the digits in each group of N.

Rhythmic quantification, the purpose of which is to produce a qualitative/aesthetic effect, is a law and evidence for music: it is to musical studies, in the following paragraph, that we leave the task of illustrating what is meant by *schematisation through rhythm*.

## THE MUSICAL RHYTHM

The history of rhythm and the history of musical rhythm coincide for the most part. Both begin in ancient Greece.

Among the Greeks, rhythm, music, poetry and dance were part of a single system, based on the rule that one long syllable had the duration of two short ones. Benveniste (1966/1971) quotes Plato's Greek definition of rhythm: 'rhythm is the order of movement'. The Platonic rhythm descends from a cosmological order of which the individual is a part and which he can re-establish – should this order be disturbed – at festivals. Rhythm is the *law of attunement* between man and the gods. Aristotle departs from this definition and considers *rhythm to derive from human action* and not from the absolute. More precisely, *mousiké* has the capacity, among other things, to activate, through rhythms, certain ethical qualities of the human soul.

## HISTORICAL LANDMARKS

In ancient times, it is mainly to Aristoxenes that one must turn to find a rhythmic theory of music. In his *Elementa rhythmica*, he places the measure of rhythmic quality in its perceptibility by man: there would be a perceptual threshold level, and it would take its morphology from the metric foot. Thesis and arsis, long phase and short phase that make up the rhythmic cell, must be in the foot in a 1:1 ratio. As Seidel (1975) clearly explains, Aristoxenes' theory is already a reflection on the moment of aesthetic reception rather than on the objective mode of existence of art: the dual possibility of the objective and subjective existence of rhythm is not yet contemplated.

In the works of St. Augustine, we find six books dedicated to rhythm: here, too, it is the principle of proportion from a numerical point of view that defines rhythm. For him too, aesthetic judgment derives from the feeling of correspondence, of *correctness*, between our perception and the event that triggers it. He distinguishes three types of rhythmic structures: elementary structures (feet); sentence-sized structures (metres and verses); stanza-sized structures (periods). But more interesting in Augustine is the theory of *latent rhythm*, of the *ratio numerorum* that is in us, in our body, in our memory, in our senses and in our reason, and that generates pleasure in man when he encounters rhythmic movements in the world. Here, rhythm seems to be conceived as descending from an experiential Gestalt.

The Middle Ages were characterised by a strong ambiguity: while, on the one hand, the measure of rhythmic unity still rested in the potential of the human voice, on the other hand, rhythmic procedures would find support in an a priori entity, the *perfectio*, founded on theological grounds that contrasted the freedom of progression and variation of musical rhythmicity.

The Renaissance, on the contrary, often leaned towards ancient times and in particular towards St. Augustine. Zarlino (1554) conceived polyphony in a very similar way as Plato did, as a complex work where words, notes and rhythms have to tune, but are in themselves autonomous. In the Baroque era, measure – equal/inequal – is the fundamental category of rhythmic theory. However, as Seidel (1975) points out, it was only a formal hypothesis at the time, which implied musical movements that were difficult to achieve.

In the eighteenth century came the theories of Johann Georg Sulzer (1720–1779) and Koch (1749–1816). Sulzer takes up the idea that symmetry exerts a special attraction on man, capable of generating pleasure: the musical object shall consider its perceiver and measure shall fit into a regular recurrence, giving rise to a coordination that is a melodic expression. Koch put this theory into technical terms and elaborated his musical phraseological theory; according to him, the optimal phrase is the one with four measures, the one that best corresponds to man's rhythmic instinct.

## TOWARDS A DOUBLE ARTICULATION

It is impossible to list here all the theories that have marked the history of music when speaking of rhythm. For the nineteenth century, think of Beethoven, who again raised the problem of the dialectic between rhythm and metre, still unresolved. This dialectic runs through Romanticism and remains still very much relevant today, as it is still debated. For example, it is taken up by Pierre Boulez (1966/1968, p. 157) who states: 'Unquestionably, it would be helpful to bring rhythm into consonance with the serial structure' to grant equal importance to rhythmic and serial structures.

Finally, following a very thorough work on African music, Simba Arom reviews the relationship between rhythm and metre in music in a very insightful article. In his definition of this relationship, metrics are seen as something that concerns the distribution of time in equal quantities – or values; rhythm, on the other hand, as the manner in which they are grouped (1992, p. 201).

In other words, the metric constitutes a continuum on which rhythm would apply as a temporal form, defined by the marks of accentuation, modification of timbres and alternation of durations. Measure would be of the order of the virtual, on which a regular recurrence inscribes a first level of rhythmic articulation; if rhythmic articulation is not in contradiction with this first level, there is no difference between rhythm and realised (*commetric*) measure; however, if, as happens in most cases, rhythm does not coincide with this first level, a second level of rhythmic (*contrametric*) organisation is established.

There would thus be a *double articulation*, responsible for the ambivalence and poignancy of rhythmic structuring, which presupposes an internal organisation of the rhythmic group and a syntax of the rhythmic groups among themselves (cf. our fourth chapter).

In Chailley's view, rhythm can only be conceived through the perception of relationships between points of support, whether divided or not, isochronous or not, and not by addition of undifferentiated parcels, whether equal or not (1979, p. 9).

There seems to be a relationship of mutual dependence between rhythm and metre, at least in music, which gives rise to periodic hierarchies, rhythmic *figures*, deeply rooted in cultural differences.

According to Jean-Jacques Nattiez (1987/1990), at least in music, the debate is rather between two notions of rhythm, one of which encompasses the metre, and another that is differentiated from it by a third component, the accent. He argues that metre can be confused with rhythm. Using the definition of rhythmic neutral level, the term rhythm basically designates an interval of time between two events, and this interval is precisely periodicity; metre and rhythm can be confused because a metrical structure possesses two qualities proper to rhythm in general, namely the interval of time, periodic and isochronous, between the underlying beats, and the larger, equally periodic and isochronous, interval of time between the returns of time, which segments the continuum of beats into isochronous units (the measures). Thus the concept of rhythm can not only designate the phenomenon of the metre but can also be applied to any element of the musical material:

– the relative duration of sounds, but also to their relations of loudness and sharpness (Vincent d'Indy, 1903); this also explains Fraisse's (1974) position that psychological analysis shows that accentual structures and temporal structures cannot be separated;

– same pitch (Beethoven, Pastoral Symphony);

– the rhythm of the melodic line (rising and descending sounds) (Willems, 1954, p. 14);

– the harmonic rhythm (succession of chords and cadences);

– even musical units of identical duration (Reicha, 1814, p. 9).

(Ibid., pp. 122–123)

If at a neutral level rhythm is for Nattiez, the articulation of the musical unfolding in different durations, at the discourse level it has to cope with metrical scansion, in different forms according to different cultures.

It is between two accentuation systems, the result of which consists of different poetic processes, that the comparison is made. This is the main idea developed by Maury Yeston, in his work *The stratification of Musical Rhythm* (1976). However, the comparison occurs between levels that do not necessarily correspond to that of rhythm and metre, as the musical object is divided into multiple hierarchical layers: background, intermediate levels and foreground. Still related to tonal and harmonic organisation, these rhythmic stratifications take into account different pitches and tones in a way that can help understand cultural differences in the perception of rhythm. As Nattiez (1987/1990, p. 138) states, rhythm is a semiological phenomenon on all levels. No matter from which perspective one considers it, rhythm must be distinguished from metre, or metre must be incorporated into rhythm, and its scope can be extended to all musical phenomena. In our culture, rhythm and metre are related. As a poetic fact, rhythm segments time; as a poetic fact, it commands gestural synchronisation; as a perceived fact, it induces levels of regularity. All the symbolic phenomena acting in whatever production – perception, repetition, differentiation, grouping, pauses, etc. – seem to contribute to the functioning of both rhythm and metre.

## MUSIC PERCEPTION

Irrespective of the debates on rhythm and metre differences encountered in poetry and which may give full insight into the ambiguity of the rhythmic phenomenon per se, if we wish to return to our hypothesis of the *preferential rooting of rhythmic grouping* in human perception, reference must be made to two fundamental texts for the application of cognitive theories to music, theories which we consider to be the only ones that take into account with sufficient fairness the relationships between the physical and the symbolic implied in rhythm. We will look precisely at the definitions of rhythm provided by John A. Sloboda in *The Musical Mind* (1985), and Fred Lerdahl and Ray Jackendoff in *A generative theory of tonal music* (1983).

According to Sloboda, the rhythmic movements of the human body and the voice form the foundation motivation for music; rhythm can be represented as a tree that makes the rhythmic intention perceivable through variations in intensity (although the listener can always impose a rhythmic grouping on a structure of regular iterations); the competence that enables the recognition of a rhythm is considered universal and innate. While Sloboda argues that rhythm ranks among the universal configurations of expression well before the appearance of musical competence in the strict sense – an opinion we fully share – we do not, however, find in this author's theoretical perspective the proposal of a true system of rhythmic preferential grouping such as in Lerdahl and Jackendoff, of which we retain, in particular, the proposal of the existence of a *temporal schematisation* underlying every expressive formulation.

Here is the *Summary of Rhythmic Features* formulated by these two authors (pp. 283–285):

(1) The grouping component expresses assign the segmentation of a piece into musical units inferred by the listener from the musical surface.
    [...]

(2) The metrical component assigns the pattern of strong and weak beats heard by the listener. Metrical accents are distinguished from phenomenal accents, which are an input to the metrical structure, and structural

accents, which are represented in time-span reduction.
[...]

(3) A group at a small or intermediate grouping level can have a strongest beat, around which other beats within the group 'cluster'.
[...]

(4) The listener hears pitch-events in the context of rhythmic units composed of a combination of metrical and grouping time-spans.
[...]

(5) In a broad sense, the function of time-span reduction is to relate rhythmic structure and pitch structure to each other.
[...]

(6) A structural downbeat represents the instantaneous confluence of a grouping boundary (often in conjunction with an overlap), a hypermetrical strong beat, and a structurally important event in time-span reduction.
[...]

(7) Prolongational reduction expresses one of the most basic rhythmic intuitions: the breathing in and out, the tensing and relaxing, inherent in the motion of pitch-events.
[...]

(8) The events contained under a prolongational branching complex can be thought of as a prolongational grouping.
[...]

(9) Time-span reduction and prolongational reduction can be in a congruent or non-congruent relation to one another.

That same feature of transversality we are pursuing is present in this approach to the rhythmic theory (complemented by the theory of 'preference rules' described in chapter 5), 'music theory begins to bridge the gap between two other capacities that have been studied extensively: visual perception and language' (ibid., p. 332).

In this regard, we feel necessary to return to the principles of the Gestalttheorie and the conception of *perception as a set of laws of dynamic and preferential organisation*. In our opinion, the Gestalttheorie is the only theoretical reflection that has so far been able to account for the interdisciplinary and, paradoxically, also the physical-symbolic complexity inherent in the rhythmic phenomenon.

## RHYTHM IN FILMS

The film environment is a privileged field for rhythmic research. By means of a syncretic musicality made up of spaces and times, rhythm guarantees the image its disconnection from its referent, from the object that constitutes its pretext. On the other hand, the idea of rhythm is inseparable from any artistic production, be it literary, pictorial, or any other, as it is first and foremost a technique of representation. Jean Mitry, in his work *The Aesthetics and Psychology of Cinema* (1990/1997), states that the rhythm of film, however, has a fundamental difference to the rhythm of sound: it does not depend on formal laws and is linear. This is equivalent to saying that it would, however, have a *narrative development*. Mitry postulates that in music rhythm is the identical found in the other, whereas in film production it is merely the analogue recognised in the dissimilar. Thus in the film image there is no right rhythm or false rhythm, if by false rhythm is meant a rhythm that would or would not conform to certain rules or fixed forms. Visual rhythm has only conditions intrinsic to the image it represents, it is a function of what is to be rhythmised. And therefore it can only be judged as a function of the specific piece of film and not by reason of some absolute principle (p. 54).

While we cannot share this ontological view of rhythm, we do appreciate the proposed conception of rhythm as a *morphological agent*, resulting from the specific constraints of the discourse in which it intervenes.

On this subject, we refer to the contribution of Francesco Maria Nappi, author of a very valuable reflection on film rhythm (1985, p. 33), in which he states that what matters most in rhythm is not the actual duration but the impression of duration, which is an internal quality and the only possible landmark, but not an established metric length. The duration is not in any way proportional to the interest and meaning of the images alone. Jean Mitry defines rhythm as a structure, but a structure that does not obey formal laws or principles that can be applied to any subject, but rather a structure, a rhythmic figuration that is solely determined by the content of the film. The film, the rhythmic figuration, is the form, and the movement is the substance of this form, and there can be no separation between the two, as Hjelmslev would also say.

## MONTAGE AND RHYTHMIC FIGURATION

Indeed, Nappi makes a distinction between *rhythmic figuration*, a subjective perception, and *rhythmic structure*, a system effect resulting from a productive intention. In *The Movement Image*, with regard to *montage*, Deleuze describes the overdetermination of duration expressed by 'movement-images' as responsible for this structure:

> *Montage is the operation which bears on the movement-images to release the whole from them, that is, the image of time. It is a necessarily indirect image, since it is deduced from movement-images and their relationship. Montage does not come afterwards, for all that. Indeed, it is necessary that the whole should be primary in a certain way, that it should be presupposed.*
> (Deleuze, 1983/2001, p. 29)

The central role of montage in the rhythmic organisation of film is one of the fundamental points of the 1920s theatre avant-garde theories, and of all of them, Sergei Ejzenstein's theory. For this author, montage is closely linked to the composition of the scene shot and exercises a dual function, one of narrative representation and, at the same time, one of image generalised through rhythm. Ejzenstein distinguishes between the rhythm that *serves the representation*, but without translating the generalised image of the event, and the rhythm in which the composition *interprets the representation*, up to the rhythm that generalises the internal content of an event, reinforcing its internal tension. The filmmaker (1963–70/2010, p. 228) classifies montage into two main types, the second of which contains the type specifically loaded with rhythmic effects:

(1) Types of Montage Classified by Semantic Sequence

  a. Montage parallel to the evolving course of the event (simple information montage);

  b. Montage parallel to the course of several sets of action ('parallel' montage);

  c. Montage parallel to perception (montage of simple comparison);

  d. Montage parallel to perception and meaning (image-forming montage);

  e. Montage parallel to ideas (concept-forming montage)... [...]

(2) Types of Montage Classified by Kinetic Sequence

   a. Metric;

   b. Rhythmic;

   c. Tonal (melodic);

   d. Overtonal;

   e. Intellectual, as a new quality in the development of overtonal montage towards significating overtones.


RHYTHMIC RELATIONS

There is a clear gap between these two types of rhythmic montage: sound film seems to have resolved it by stripping rhythm of its didactic rhythmic functions in relation to time, and emphasising the responsibilities of plastic rhythmicity and composition. In this case, rhythm serves first and foremost to express an *internal tension*, which does not necessarily correspond to figurative entities.

Also, a complex series of *rhythmic relations* runs between music and performance, from chord to counterpoint, according to the scansion principle decided by the composition: but the essential thing is that both chord and counterpoint can be attached either to the form of content (*semantic montage* according to Ejzenstein), or to the form of expression (*kinetic montage*, again according to Ejzenstein), or to both, depending on the director's instructions.

This leads again, in our opinion, to the question already raised of envisaging a mechanism of double articulation, for an in-depth understanding of rhythm Ejzenstein's so-called *vertical* montage ultimately exploits the different coded forms to produce rhythmic effects linked to the content of the representation, provoking *synaesthetic* perceptual effects, whereby one of the senses (sight, hearing) is charged with transmitting potentialities to all the others. It is the *mimetic* aspect of rhythm, made possible by its figural pertinence, before its figurative one.

## RHYTHM IN THEATRE

Rhythm in theatre, however, covers a wider area than that occupied by montage. From the avant-gardes of the 1920s, and from Ejzenstein's early works for theatre, to Mejerch'old, Brecht, Piscator, these two concepts (or, rather, techniques), rhythm and montage, have been related and studied, if not used, in very similar ways. However, we would like to treat them separately here, without omitting their inevitable interactions.

A very detailed definition of rhythm in theatre is provided by Patrice Pavis in his *Dictionary of the Theatre: Terms, Concepts, and Analysis* (1987/1998, p. 314):

> *Rhythm is present at every level of the production, not just in the way the performance unfolds in time and its duration.*

And under 'Rhythm', he identifies seven levels where a rhythmic structure can be recognised (pp. 314–315):

A. Enunciation of reading

Even when a text is given a 'flat' and 'expressionless' reading in a neutral voice, rhythm is already at work, as soon as the speaker takes a position on his utterances.

Rhythm is therefore always present to introduce those discontinuities that make communication possible.

B. Rhythmic oppositions

In the performance, the rhythm can be felt in the perception of binary effects: silence/speech, fast/slow, meaningful/meaningless, stressed/unstressed, foregrounded/backgrounded, determinacy/indeterminacy. Rhythm is not confined to the enunciation of a text, but applies to the visual arts as well; Adolphe Appia, for instance, speaks of 'rhythmic space' in relation to stage design. Edward Gordon Craig makes rhythm an essential component of theatre art, 'the very essence of dance.'

Rhythm introduces a principle of alternation and variation present in all *mise-en-scène* codes and is often called upon to coordinate them.

C. Gestus and trajectory

The search for the gestus and the basic arrangement and blocking of the actors on stage, the composition of groups in tableaux or subgroups – such are some of the actors' gestural and proxemic effects. Their movements on stage become a physical representation of the rhythm of the production. Rhythm is the visualisation of time in space, a writing of the body and its contextualisation in the stage and fictional space.

In this sense, it identifies with a deixis, with a vector of focus.

The various rhythmic pertinences pointed out so far by Pavis derive from the *plasticity* of the performance. The following are derived first and foremost from its *narrative structuring*. Plasticity and narrative structuring are intertwined with the aim of managing the viewer's attention.

D. Breaks

The practice of using breaks, discontinuity, alienation-effects – all devices that are frequently employed in contemporary art – favours the perception of pauses in the performance; this makes the syncopated rhythm all the more apparent.

E. Voice

Voice has become the extreme modaliser of the entire text; the intonational colouration and its ability to relate verbal and non-verbal, explicit and implicit aspects make it 'the phonic expression of social evaluation' (Bakhtin in Todorov, 1981, p. 74).

F. Narrative rhythm

All the various rhythms of the stage systems of performance (the result of which forms the mise-en-scène) can be read only within the framework of the fabula. The rhythm recovers its function in structuring time in episodes, speeches, series of monologues or stichomythia, scene changes.

G. Overall rhythm of mise-en-scène

Within the narrative framework that gives rhythm to the fabula, that 'electric current' that connects the various materials of performance as described by J. Honzl (1940), arise the specific rhythms of all the stage systems (lighting, gestuality, music, costumes, etc.). Each stage system evolves according to its own rhythm; the perception of differences in synchronisation, the different shifters, the hierarchies between signifying systems; all this is part of the (logical and narrative) ordering of the mise-en-scène by the spectator.

As we can see in this summary, rhythm is at the heart of the manifestations of theatrical communication, both those that are related to the plastic function and those that descend from the narrative function. Rhythm is the constitutive act of the productive movement and also – and Pavis does not emphasise this enough – of the *receptive moment*.

*From dramatic literature to the mise-en-scène.*

For theatre, rhythm is first and foremost the medium that allows it to move beyond the stage of *dramatic literature* to which it has long been stuck. It rests, as we well know, on certain physiological foundations that the actor cannot disregard: respiration, heart rhythm, circadian rhythms; through the actor, the performed work nevertheless experiences a rhythmic investment, so much so that it can become the actual purpose of the performance, which is increasingly common in contemporary staging. According to Pavis (ibid., p. 314),

> *Contemporary mise-en-scène, whether by the Théâtre du Soleil (MNOUCHKINE), by VITEZ or by DELBÉE, seems fascinated by the possibility of changing the perception of a text through experiments with rhythm.*

But rhythm has always been one of the building blocks of theatrical dialogue, when not of the mise-en-scène. And if research on rhythm is nowadays explicit, it is easy to trace the effects of repetition in any dramatic writing, which act on the reader/spectator in a more or less evident manner according to the intention of the author, the director, the performer, and according to the attention of the receiver. As Pierre Larthomas (1980) very pertinently writes, each utterance does not contain only one rhythm, but various rhythms that combine their effects but may also oppose each other; the study of these rhythms makes it possible to define the rhythm of an utterance and, more specifically, of a dramatic dialogue (p. 310).

Larthomas also distinguishes between *rhythm, number* and *time*: if rhythm is essentially the effect of repetition, number concerns the length and overlapping of different elements of a sentence: there can therefore be number without rhythm. On the other hand, time is universal, it designates the speed, more or less great, at which a scene is acted out, and which descends from an inevitable effect of interpretation.

The reproach we address to Larthomas' remarks is that they are in theory simple and correct, but limited to the verbal code in its written or spoken form. We are, on the contrary, well aware that the responsibilities of rhythm in theatre are wider in scope, and that they participate in all the code systems involved in the representation.

Starting from this reflection, we consider it appropriate to take a look, at least from a closer distance, at the intentions of a discipline of theatrical origin too often wrongly counted among esoteric practices: *eurythmy*.

Eurythmy, which originated at the beginning of the twentieth century from Jacques Dalcroze's work on the body, was taken over in the form of therapy by Rudolf Steiner, and is still practised today by doctors trained according to Steiner's principles. It consists of a form of total expression that plays with the human body as with an orchestra, combining gestures, music, poetry, colours, in search of harmony. We clearly find here a reconnection with the deep sense of rhythm in ancient Greece, coordination of dance, gymnastics and choreography. Again, one of the fundamental exercises for establishing rhythmic measurement is the march, the foot raised to walk, determining three phases with different periods.

For Steiner (1966), eurythmy performs a therapeutic function: but this function is conceivable thanks to the conviction of a possible correspondence between man and the universe around him, between proprioceptive and exteroceptive factors. The rhythmic consonance used in some performances, which are almost theatrical, can allow this *harmonic junction*. The basic teaching of eurythmy, stripped of all mystical connotations, introduces and imposes – we believe – a semiotic reinterpretation of rhythm considered as a *mediator between affection, perception and action*.

## MONTAGE AS A RHYTHMIC DEVICE

Finally, with regard to *montage* – a privileged technique of 'surface' rhythmics – in theatre, we suggest considering the following problematic issues:

(1) Montage as a discursive technique, a necessary tool for all types of writing, based on a syntactic or semantic criterion of textual coherence;

(2) Montage as a strategy, a tool for modelling the path of the observer-actant, a solution that aims to predetermine the correspondence between the focalisations set by the enunciator and the focalisations implemented by the listener;

(3) Montage as a mode of discursive manipulation, as a persuasive game that works on the combination of the different materials of expression involved in the mise-en-scène (light, sounds, objects, words, bodies, gestures), both individually, code by code, and at the level of the syncretic fusion of codes, both within the isolated scene, and in the logic of the concatenation of the scenes that cover the total time of the performance;

(4) Montage as a cohesive and distributive dynamic with some consequences both on the level of a typology of enunciation and on the level of reception, where the suggested point of view is opposed to the freedom of an unconstrained point of view;

(5) Finally, montage as an anchor, a strong construction of the theatrical spectator's point of view, at the same time free and constrained, almost as much as that of the cinematic spectator.

This premise illustrated, we will now try to arrive at an acceptable definition of theatrical montage. At the level of the *form of expression*, rhythm and montage seem to us to be very similar structures. Rhythm can be defined as a pragmatic device, a productive–receptive practice to be found in the manifestation of discourse, at the intersection between a theory of reception and a theory of manifestation. In this sense, it is an 'empty grid' that is applied to the figurative density to control its distribution and linearisation, and ensure the continuity and pragmatic effectiveness of the intended focalisations.

The question of rhythm becomes more delicate when we come to that last level that refers to the *form of the content*, and when we try to conceive it as a fundamental morphology. Conceived as an orientation grid, a quantification/ aspectualisation of the narrative programme – rhythm can be considered as a process control system that organises the dynamics, both temporal and volitional, of narrative expectation.

Semantically, montage performs the same function, and in this sense, also maintains a position as a non-specific code. By conditioning content selection operations, montage as a discursive structure determines the value of each utterance according to its position and its relation to other utterances. It acts as a constraint governing the coherence of the discourse as a whole.

Also with regard to the relationship between the plane of content and the plane of expression, and thus with regard to the project of reception and the modelling of a virtual spectator implied by the performance-text, montage functions as the articulation of a semi-symbolic semiotics, at both synchronic and diachronic levels. From a set of plastic oppositions (here/there, inside/ outside, high/low, light/dark, coherent/dispersed, still/moving, etc.), which articulate graphic, volume, spatial and light contrasts, and which are both topological and visual, montage operates on the realised focalisations, on the displacements and figurativisations of the observer–actant, on his processes of spatialisation, temporisation and actorisation. These categories will correspond to one another on the level of content, where pairs of oppositions of the continuous/discontinuous, whole/part, centred/decentred, oriented/not oriented, defined/undefined type are activated.

*Rhythmic semiotics*, montage can be configured as a *transversal system*, called upon to account for the ways in which the viewer of the *mise-en-scène* is invested by the different combinations of rhythmic categories, on which the composition of the discourse, and, to a large extent, its aesthetic intention and pragmatic efficacy, depends.

## RHYTHM IN COMMUNICATION

Discussing rhythm in communication is a task that is as generic as it is necessary. It is generic because we are thinking of an extremely broad communication mix, from more traditional media activities (advertising in the press, TV, radio, cinema) to urban marketing activities (out of home and guerrilla), to digital marketing activities in the whole varied palette of social networks, websites and blogs, within chats and forums, or in video apps. It is necessary, because it is a consequence of the extreme crowding of platforms, of all kinds, and therefore with an indispensable need for matrices of a strategic nature to coordinate the different types of intervention and communicational presence.

Regardless of the interface used, rhythm in communication calls into question different levels of pertinence:

(1) The management of contents and their visual surfaces

(2) The way users are involved, the structuring of their relational journey

(3) The planning of presence in the media arena, the modes of visibility, its dosage.

As understood here, rhythm is a *device*, i.e. an active, performative instrument for relating the communicational proposal to the effects it is likely to solicit on its receiver: it therefore touches on real issues related to the effectiveness of policies, investments, positioning and the support that communication gives them.

We will address these three different levels in detail below in order to bring out the relevance that taking the rhythmic matrix into account has for each one of them.

## THE MANAGEMENT OF CONTENTS AND THEIR VISUAL SURFACES

We consider here how much the distribution of a content can influence the attention span of its audience and, on the other hand, how much a Gestalt management of vivid interfaces will allow to draw on the relevance they can assume if structured according to the principles of 'good form'.

The issue of content has become crucial when, along with the expansion of digital marketing, very high competition for visitor retention on web pages has emerged, parallel to the need of traditional distribution to retain that same visitor within its physical spaces. Thus, the word 'content' no longer refers only to themes developed around a given subject (be it that of a commercial, or institutional, or even personal brand) but any element that could be useful to capture users for a minimum time, if possible not just any user. Competitions, parallel information, services, games – in this sense anything is virtually content, as long as it can be used to build up what is called 'lead generation', i.e. a list of potential or actual people interested in one's communication proposal.

And so the rhythm that is capable of managing the fruition of these contents according to a preordained design becomes crucial in distributing them according to groups that invest mechanisms of simple expectation and then, as the phenomenon repeats itself, of confident expectation, as it is well demonstrated both by the trailer of the serial fiction and the series themselves, which not surprisingly are mainly distributed on the net, i.e. the place where the user subject can activate personalised modes of intensification or de-intensification of contact.

Concentration (of contents) and expansion are the principles underlying this mode of management, to which corresponds a consequent involvement of the interfaces which will follow the same principles of alternation – pauses and peaks of concentration, latencies and events – through the use of plastic categories of reference: eidetic and chromatic, first of all, where the two-dimensionality of the image will allow the development of a journey with alternating peaks. This is even more true, of course, in the case of audiovisuals, where the modulation of the sound, in addition to the montage, will also influence the construction of the expectation to which the content leads.

These are effects of planning and pressure, as we well know, but also, and purely, of a rhythmic conception of experience, according to a grouping of events which must tactically respect the strategic management of the whole.

An example of this is the storytelling of the TIM 2017–2018 campaign, (https://www.youtube.com/watch?v=oulsbb6BLDY), which is part of the already numerous Transmedia branding interventions to address and deal with what is, in our opinion, the central issue of a complex communication strategy: namely, the transformative mechanisms that allow the initial script, the 'zero' content, to spread and structure itself, to expand across different forms of media, achieving the primary objectives of reach, longevity and intensity (see Tenderich, 2014). We refer to those turning points that represent the articulations of a rising rhetoric, destined to contaminate more and more channels of communication by amplifying its imaginative reach. They are content articulations on which the strategic structure of the transmedia operation depends; they are both the support of its reticularity but also the opening of alternative realisation options that refer them to a vocation, both semiotic and sociological, of an anticipatory nature.

Like any narrative form, transmedia branding is a rhythmic structure, both in terms of expression and content. Its structure and plot are based on intervals, groupings and repetitions, giving rise to phenomena of retention and protention: a guiding thread which, in the case of the aforementioned TIM, allowed the plot to run coherently for two years, moving from the famous electroswing dancer (https://www.youtube.com/watch?v=qbenUjM-fzs) protagonist of the network to Spiderman and Star Wars, through different media interfaces (online and offline), in pursuit of a consequent transformation of the content itself.

## THE WAYS RECIPIENTS ARE INVOLVED

As we introduced above, transmediality is today the most crucial form of involvement of potential recipients, and also the one that is most supported by a rhythmic framework. This supports the expansion of the script by giving it an articulation that relies on the formants that underpin figurativity.

It is a strategy of a rhythmic nature, inviting the conception of a reticular mechanism that decides the syntax through which a brand/communication subject can evolve: the surface syntax, or storyline, includes intratextual transformations, first of all, and then of course intertextual ones, in order to constantly regenerate the attentional exercise. It is a system of equivalences between formants in which the transformation calls into question a mythical system: whether in relation to variants of the system itself, to other myths, or more simply to the syntagms that compose it.

The 'movement form' of rhythm (Benveniste, 1966/1971) is expressed by recursive phenomena that lead to a tensive solidarity allowing the interrelation of categorised sensory data and transmedial encodings, bringing into play for the potential recipient a technique of (1) communication, (2) control, (3) power (Salmon, 2017). This is how, thanks to the rhythmic structure, storytelling interprets the semiotic function in a binding manner, creating the mutual presupposition between form and content. Thus, the storytelling interprets the semiotic function in a binding way through the rhythmic structure, creating a mutual presupposition between form and content.

The 'storyworld' is therefore a second-level entity that requires narrative/assembly competence in the ideal reader. This is how an active creation of belief is exercised, where the condensation/expansion of rhythmic groups stages the profound opposition between singularity and multiplicity: for example, in the TIM storytelling of the period cited, it is the figurative matrix of swing that constructs a relationship between sensory apprehension and the values invested in the figurative discourse.

## PLANNING PRESENCE IN THE MEDIA ARENA

Transmedia fictionality, a pillar of contemporary media planning, when it does not happen directly through automation (but ultimately also through the latter if we think of the meticulous programming of the keywords with which content is indexed), implies an intratextual and syntagmatic transformation. This is done through the selection of touchpoints that mark the initial and final states according to what Greimas himself (1983/1987) called 'an algorithm of transformation'.

These points of contact are three in number: the 'characters', i.e. the actors who cumulate an actantial role with a thematic role, and thus an argumentative and strategic position in the story and a narrative component; the 'community', i.e. the relationship to the public of the recipients involved, an actantial and thematic figure not necessarily consensual, with a strong tensive relationship in relation to the possible reception of the contents; and finally, what Robert Pratten ('The three Cs of Transmedia storytelling', 2011) calls 'convenience', that is, the narrative format that can have very different syntactic structures, linear or branched, dynamic, open or participative, establishing different levels of possible inclusion and response.

Nevertheless, following a rhythmic logic even in planning thought, belief (and with it commitment) is confirmed as an active creation, which develops by condensation/expansion of rhythmic groups, according to a profound opposition which alternates between singularity and multiplicity on the plastic level. Planning is first and foremost the holding of the interaction, which is logically based on the *shared* belief.

If media planning was traditionally based on a predefined *programming* strategy (based on the regularity and predictability of the response/encounter with the potential media user/target), today the rhythmic system increasingly resembles its opposite, i.e. this adjustment regime, based on sensitivity (cf. Landowski, 2005) and on a provisional competence, redefined from time to time according to the end-user's increasingly transversal media consumption paths, thus making the potential of the rhythmic device much more circumscribed, its use and effectiveness much more tactical than strategic.

# 3

# THE SEMIOTIC APPROACH

Before tackling the conceptual definition of rhythm that should allow – or at least we hope – to best resolve the difficult synthesis between the approach of the theory of perception and that of a theory of linguistic production, it seems important to us to question the *contributions* and *limits* of the semiotic approach.

We will therefore attempt not only to gradually develop a definition of rhythm as a *device* but also to verify and extend the core hypothesis underlying the present work: rhythm – understood as a constraint – represents the *invariant underlying the process of transcoding*[1] of two texts of a different semiotic nature (i.e. which do not have the same matter of expression).

Although concurrent with textual information, rhythmic information can nevertheless be independent of it: this implies that its meaning must be sought in the *organisation* of the signifying arrangement, in the structures governing the manifestation. We will first try to explain how a *rhythmic configuration* is structured, i.e. a grid of syntactic and semantic distribution that can be the common and invariant support of different forms of discourse.

## EARLY DEFINITIONS

According to a shared understanding, rhythm consists of an activity marked by intervals of time (or space, when it comes to visual rhythms). In their

---

1 In *Semiotics and language: an analytical dictionary* by Greimas and Courtés (1978/1983, p. 348), transcoding is defined as 'the operation' (or set of operations) by which an element or a meaningful set is transposed from one code into another, from one language into another language.

*Semiotic and language: an analytical dictionary*, Greimas and Courtés (1978/1983, p. 264) define rhythm as an *expectation*, i.e. as a given type of temporal investment, aided by:

> [...] *the aspect of inchoateness) of the modality of wanting-to-be as applied to the recurrent interval between groups of asymmetrical elements, reproducing the same formation.*

Similarly, albeit using a different terminology, Christian Metz (1971/1974, p. 220) states that:

> *A rhythmical scheme – even if one could, and even if one ought to analyze it as a purely relational form, as an abstract relation of measurable dimensions – is an intrinsically temporal phenomenon. If this is forgotten, it would still be a scheme, but no longer a rhythmical one.*

Partially contradictory to each other (Metz's formulation does neither consider aspectuality, nor volition), these two semiotic definitions of rhythm that we have just recalled still remain somewhat vague and unsatisfactory, as they only pay attention to temporality as a relevant feature of the rhythmic paradigm: what they emphasise in this case is therefore a *non-specificity* of rhythm, which leads us to attempt to provide a more comprehensive explanation; above all one capable of accounting for the assumed extensibility of this type of space-time organisation.

Let us then try to think of rhythm as a system, i.e. as a structure composed of differential correlations: as such, it represents a code, and thus a rule, a mechanism of responsible transformation, which can be recognised at the level of both expression and content: what interests us here in particular is the possibility of the *persistence of a form of rhythmic content through the mutation of the materials of expression.*

According to Benveniste (1966/1971), rhythm is first and foremost a *form of movement*. Now, if among the relevant traits of the rhythmic code we have first of all identified temporality, we must add another imperative: the code can be recognised as a configuration, a kind of matrix, of design, of pre-narrative model, which is inscribed in the *spatio-temporal* nature[2] of the event, proposing a reading grid. Every human experience, active and perceptual, inevitably has a *temporal character*, governed by an order that can be represented on a *spatial vector*, called in semiotics the *axis of perspectivity*. Any structure

---

2 Space-time is not a form of content; the perceptual nature of space-time remains an inherent difficulty, and an unresolved issue.

that realises regularities, obeying certain rules of perspective, certain strategies that control the orderly arrangement of points on a line, defined by the obligation to respect a direction and a determined *before/after* order, can become a predictive model.

Clearly, whatever the event, it must be put into perspective and represented in space-time, in order to interpret it. Spatio-temporal localisation thus becomes the first problem for an analysis of the *form of experience*, i.e. the way in which spatial and temporal categories intersect to structurally organise the event and to create the conditions for its eventual *rhythmic repetition*.

It is in this way that the assimilation of rhythm to a *configuration*, starting with Benveniste's (1966/1971) lexicological reflection, sets the conditions for a semiotics of time, but also of space, overdetermined by rhythm. This type of semiotics, which would seek to account for the form of perception, phenomenal form or form of sensual experience, has yet to be created: we will try to make our contribution in this regard.

## CONFIGURATION

How is the *rhythmic configuration* organised? From a semiotic point of view (Greimas & Courtés 1978/1983, pp. 49–51), a configuration constitutes a micro-universe of narratives that is autonomous, both semantically and syntactically, with respect to the context in which it is embedded. A configuration represents the temporal and spatial necessity that governs representation, the caesura of intervals between events, *operational time* – as Piaget (1946/1969) understands it, which superimposes on *perceptual time* the strong and quantifiable logic of its causality. In this way, on the level of discursive syntax, the figures must account, through their distribution, for the progressive construction of the *effect of rhythm* through which the utterance subordinates the entire textual mise-en-scène to a (necessarily normalised, i.e. aspectualised[3]) temporal isotopy.

However, in the sense in which we understand it, a rhythmic configuration is the neutral, not yet figurative pattern of the arrangement of an event-theme in space-time. But, in order to have a configuration, it is necessary to maintain a coherence with the consecutive logic that decides on the arrangement and quantity of the relevant units, i.e. the events of conjunction and disjunction,[4]

---

3 Aspectuality is an overdetermination of temporality, as a result of sèmes that allow an utterance to be represented in terms of process.

4 Cf. the semio-narrative theory of A. J. Greimas: it speaks of conjunction and disjunction between subject and object of value.

and the intervals between events. This logic, entirely responsible for the shaping of discourse, refers back to what we call the *rhythmic device*. The rhythmic device ensures that the syntagmas follow one another according to an order of presupposition that will be, at the same time, of spatial and temporal distribution, in order to capture the receiver's attention and to orientate his or her cognitive thymic and evaluative trajectories.

## THE RHYTHMIC GROUP

What we need to do now is to provide a preliminary description of the unit cell of rhythmic configuration, i.e. the underlying microstructure of what, figuratively covered at the level of discursive manifestation, is recognisable narratively as a *rhythmic group*.

The rhythmic group can be defined as a *unit of information delimited by two intervals*, containing a minimum *triphasic* pattern, describing a curve, ascending at the moment of the inchoative pulse, durative at the moment of culminating tension and descending in the relaxation phase. This scheme describes the alternation of states of tension/distension on the content level on which euphoric/dysphoric investments can be made.

A rhythmic configuration requires the existence of at least two groups. Regardless of its position within the discourse, the group, like the configuration that supports it, possesses a level of autonomy and a faculty of inter-textual migration that allows it to be associated with a *motif*, 'a figurative type of unit which therefore possesses a meaning that is independent of its functional signification with respect to the narrative as a whole within which it takes place' (Greimas & Courtés, 1978/1983, p. 199).

The two events presupposed by the rhythmic group are separated by an interval (non-event) that is the place of silence (discursive) and expectation (narrative). Within each event (sound, visual, narrative...) a phenomenon of alternation in three movements is produced, in which empty spaces can be called *pauses*: the threshold of the event, and of the phase within the event, is defined by the inscription of a point of view within the narrative movement, which is defined as an *observer actant*.[5]

How long can a pause last? What is the period between events within a given configuration? The arbiter of the question is that kind of *focus* inscribed

---

5 According to Greimas and Courtés (1986, p. 156) the observer actant is a place prepared by the enunciator, and a major element of the reality effect.

in the discourse and independent of the instance of enunciation, responsible for the aspectual dynamic.

## THE ASPECTUAL CONSTRAINT

Valéry states that rhythm is to time as a crystal is to an amorphous environment (Valéry, 1973/2000, p. 43). This reflection leads us to set three major research directions regarding rhythm that the aspectual 'constraint' will help us determine:

- the definition of rhythm as a *break in the symmetry* of time;
- the relation of *opposition* between rhythm and time;
- the *rhythmic organisation*, rhythm as a *crystal* embedded in amorphous temporal continuity.

In this perspective, the question of a minimal definition of the rhythmic phenomenon is articulated according to a more complex vision, that of rhythm as a tensive configuration, as a strategy for controlling the temporality of perception with the aim of directing its passionate transformations. In this sense, we will speak of the aspectual intervention as the relation between two levels of organisation: the syntactic-discursive level and the underlying-semantic level.

## GUILLAUME AND PIAGET

We thus come to the *relation between rhythm and time*. We will look at two authors from very different, though almost contemporary, backgrounds, Gustave Guillaume and Jean Piaget.

Piaget distinguishes two orders of temporality.[6] The first, called *intuitive time*, linked to immediate perception, to simple relations of succession and duration, concerns only the quantitative definition; the second, called *operational time*, which is qualitative in nature, intervenes by transforming relations into operations to the point of constructing an intellectual schematism that is the result of coordination activity. *Operational time* is thus, for Piaget, the

---

6 This distinction is further developed in Piaget (1946/1969).

organisation of disconnected minimal actions into regulatory movements, and finally into groupings with logical organisation.

By a surprising coincidence, Guillaume introduces the notion of chronogenesis (cf. Guillaume, 1929): it is an operation of thought that strives to set up time through the grammatical support of the verbal category, thus rejoining the idea of operational time.

Just as logical grouping represents, after the stages of rhythm and, the extreme stage of the cognitive movement of psychic life (including temporal representation), so time represented in the grammatical sense (mode and aspect) appears as a form of construction of elementary human experience, of learning, of perceptual processing.

Behind the notion of operational time, no matter whether from a linguistic or psychological context, we always find an operation of content, an important conceptual reality, which allows us to think of the temporal flow as a figuration, translatable into a scheme, that is, indeed, *operational*. We shall later see what consequences arise from this. For now, suffices it to say that the relation between rhythm and time requires us to define a 'general morphology of mental life' – according to Piaget's definition in his seminal article that entrusts rhythm with the role of basic structure of psychic life (cf. Piaget, 1942).

We therefore attempt to take the *event* as the minimum unit of reflection, defining it as the minimum experience of space and time. If it is true, on the one hand, that the psychological event descends from a binary periodicity consisting of two alternating phases, and, on the other, that this periodicity is translated in language into a tension represented by the verbal form and the coordination of time, manner and aspect, then, as suggested earlier, we can begin to consider rhythm as a *micro-configuration*.

## PERCEPTUAL AND OBJECTIFIED MORPHOLOGY

Capable of conditioning the nature of the event, rhythmic micro-configuration manifests itself in a balance that would result from the encounter or *'interaction' between an objectified morphology and a perceptual morphology* (as in touch), and it is this very encounter that would permit the recognition of the balance/unbalance, if not an adjustment between the two.

Now, when we speak of time, we think of Guillaume's *time of existence* ($T'$) and *spatial time* ($T''$). When we speak of rhythm, we indicate the *nature* ($T'''$) and the *unfolding of the event* ($T'''$), i.e. its aspectual forms. Let us illustrate this with the use of an example; consider the verb/to forget/.

With respect to $T'''$, /to forget/, is imperfective, it has no limits (neither beginning nor end), except when we attribute an object to it/to *forget* someone, something/. If we bring in an aspectuality of this verb ($T'''$), we will have, among other possibilities:

a. he is beginning *to forget* (inchoative);

b. he is *forgetting* (durative);

c. he stops *forgetting* (terminative).

Time intervenes in the pure verbal tension and simultaneously indicates different perspectives on the evolution of the event.

In this regard, we should keep in mind that elemental action needs equal and opposite regulation to be a signifier: each verbal form envisages an alternative sequel that allows the mobile equilibrium to assert itself and the cognitive operation to reveal itself. These considerations give rise to some opposite semantic developments:

a') he stops *remembering*;

b') he is *remembering*;

c') he is beginning to *remember*.

The possibilities (a), (b) and (c), as well as (a'), (b') and (c'), are in a relation of mutual presupposition: what comes first semantically is virtually contained in what follows, and vice versa.

The iteration that, by definition, creates rhythm must therefore be considered, within the regulating module of rhythm itself, as an action potentially contained in its aspectual *pattern*. In this sense, it is true that *there is no rhythm without iteration*, but the iterative phenomenon can also only be virtual: it is therefore possible to consider that there is a presence of rhythm, even within a single *pattern*.

In this hypothesis, each aspectual determination – a point of view *relative* to the scene represented – could be contemplated as the fragment of a more complex rhythmic structure, fully realisable and recognisable, only at the level of discursive configuration, where the verb-event interacts with the other parts of the discourse.

## ASPECTUALITY AND THE RHYTHMIC DEVICE

Rhythm, however, is more than the organised structure we have seen manifested in aspectual expressions: just like Valéry's 'crystal', rhythm is the perceptive result of a complex morphology. Temporal, spatial and actoral aspectuality collaborate in the functioning of rhythm as a device, each according to its own domain of intervention:

- The temporal aspectuality, the most immediate, decides the *consecutio temporum*, the extent and intensity, the order, duration and frequency of a manifestation;
- The spatial aspectuality intervenes in the plasticity, proxemics and iconic dynamics of paths;
- The actoral aspectuality determines the point of view through which the actor is represented, the montage of behavioural elements, the interaction realised in the polemical-contractual exchanges.

## THE GENERATION OF RHYTHM

On the semiotic level, we can say that rhythm concerns the underlying relation of the preconditions of signification (with the tension/laxity opposition as a universal semantic axis) subsequently transformed into utterances of narrative syntax, and then on the surface level of syntax and discursive semantics, where rhythm manifests itself through the subject of the utterance.

We can then delineate an outcome of the *generative path of rhythm*[7] that justifies the primary definition we have provided: that of being both an aspectual *configuration* and a form of *pregnance**. But rhythm is also, first and foremost, in the order of the generative stratification of signification, a *self-regulating module*. The metaphor of the crystal proposed by Valéry continues to seem very appropriate.

The inner rhythm, what Piaget (1942) called morphogenetic, corresponds to a simple pattern of action that testifies to the adaptation of the subject of the perception to environmental changes, to an experiential *Gestalt* neither acquired nor autonomous with respect to cognitive structures, to a compensation of external provocations. As an attempt made by the subject to resolve

---

7 Based on the generative path of signification described by the Greimasian semiotic theory.
  *Note of the translator: the French term 'prégnance' is difficult to put into English; in the official translation of René Thom's book *Semio Physics: A Sketch* (1988/1990), this term is translated as *pregnance*, although it is a rather flat translation. For ease of reference, we will use the term *pregnance* also in this book. For the reader's information, the original term from which the French term is also derived is the German *Prägnanz*.

his own internal tensions, rhythm exerts a periodic balancing action in this phase that alternates with antagonistic phases, introducing a principle of discontinuity with respect to temporal continuity.

If, on the one hand, rhythm proposes the first grounding condition of a perceptual situation, on the other, Gestal theory (*Gestalttheorie*) recognises its poignant existence through the subject's natural propensity to group isolated elements, to form an ordered structure that allows a primary configuration of the perceivable to be identified. These two aspects seem fundamental to us: a passive situation on the underlying level (rhythm as *iteration*), and an active situation on the following level (rhythm as *grouping*). In both cases, we are talking about a process that interests us as a *strategy for controlling* perception as well as action.

On the level of narrative syntax, we believe it is possible to invest the profound opposition between continuity and discontinuity inherent in euphoric and dysphoric values in actantial structures. The two movements, passive and active, of iteration and grouping, must then be re-read in the light of the sense effects determined by the modalisers of the narrative programmes. Rhythm, a device of cohesion, a tendency towards equilibrium (even if it is a mobile equilibrium), through repetition (iterated conjunction/disjunction), provokes sensations, *pathemic movements*. The narrativity of the semiotic model is made up, as we know, of tensions and returns to equilibrium followed by distensions; only the transformation of a precarious stasis produces a story.[8]

At this level, as a syntactic organisation of a *concatenation* of narrative programmes that serves as an intermediary between an inchoative will, a disjunctive expectation (the interval) and finally a conjunction that concatenates the new narrative programme, rhythm appears as a *syntactic device* capable of managing passionate articulations while guaranteeing narrative tension. Iteration then arranges the narrative programmes in a presuppositional order; there is iteration, and thus rhythm, because our memory is active.

In the transition from the semio-narrative level to the discursive level, rhythm can be described as an abstract configuration (present on the level of discursive semantics) capable of translating passionate thematisations, unresolved tensions, simulacra that nevertheless imply a dynamic scope: as a thematic-figurative form, it represents a kind of distributive network, abstract enough to encompass the isotope figures that compose it, and at the same time

---

8 'Narrative discourse appears then to be a locus of the figurative representations of the different forms of human communication, produced from tension, and of returns to equilibrium' (Greimas & Courtés 1978/1983, p. 204).

binding enough in terms of space-time to already constitute a narrative framework. Through their distribution, the figures must subsequently account for the progressive construction of the rhythm effect in the utterance, subordinating the entire *mise-en-scène* of the text to a temporal isotopy.

We therefore reiterate that a rhythmic configuration is for us the *neutral pattern of the arrangement of an event-theme in space-time*; as a principle of organisation determined on the basis of the recognition of an iteration of semantic and/or syntactic traits, we can speak of *rhythmic isotopy*, which becomes configuration when the syntagmas concerned are *held* according to a determined and *traceable* concatenation.

## EXPECTATION

Let us now return to the specificity of the rhythmic structure. To us, the decisive trait seems to be the representation of *expectation*.[9] We understand *expectation* as a discursive and narrative phenomenon.

Introducing discontinuity within the uniform duration, alternating successive micro-events as recurrence of the simultaneous, expectation reveals the *pathemical sense effect* for which the rhythmic configuration is responsible. It serves above all to explain that concept, perhaps still unclear, of the *autonomous* narrativity of the rhythmic group.

## SIMPLE EXPECTATION AND FIDUCIARY EXPECTATION

We will distinguish two types of expectation: a first one, internal to the phases that make up the rhythmic group, and a second one, relative to the configuration as a whole, that is, the expectation that lies between one group and the other. The first one was called *simple expectation* by Greimas (1983/1987, p. 150): he defines it as that which connects a subject with an object of value

> *[...] simple expectation concerns first of all a modalization of the subject, which we can characterize as /wanting-to-be-conjoined/.*
> *[...] Thus, along with the passions of action [...] we encounter*

---

9 'The concept of rhythm can also be defined in terms of expectation (C. Zilberberg, following P. Valéry)' (Greimas & Courtés, 1978/1983, p. 113).

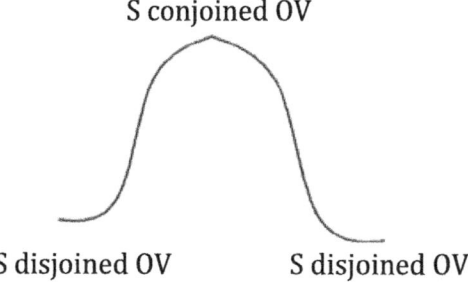

**Fig. 1. Simple Expectation.**

> *here a passion of being acted upon, that is, a passion in the classical, etymological sense of the word.*

We use this concept of expectation to describe the pattern of a group and to explain its intra-phasic cohesion, measured aspectually by the observer actant. Simple expectation draws an energy curve marked by the changes in the intensity of the tension created by the pause/silence spaces[10] during which one waits (Fig. 1).

Greimas provides a further definition of expectation, called *fiduciary expectation*.

> *Actually the subject's expectation is not a simple wish; it is inscribed against a backdrop of confidence: The subject of state "thinks it can count" on the subject of doing to realize "its expectations" and/or its "rights." If the contractual nature of the relation that gives rise to the "rights" is obvious, the obligational nature of the fact of expecting, "considering (that which is desired) as having to be realized," also appears as soon as one scratches beneath the lexematic surface. [...] We cannot speak here of a true contract (which, as we know, engages both "contracting" parties) but rather of a contract of confidence, or a pseudocontract. We could perhaps consider it an imaginary contract, for at its conclusion – or rather its recognition – the subject of doing is in no way engaged; The subject's deontic modalization is the product of the "imagination" of the subject of state. (Ibid., pp. 151–152)*

In a second figure, we will illustrate our application of this definition to the rhythmic scheme, recalling that confidence in the realisation of the event can

---

10 In this regard, see the very interesting contribution made by Delas (1991).

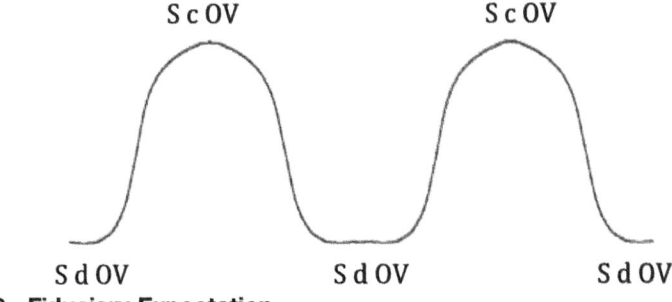

**Fig. 2. Fiduciary Expectation.**

be either spontaneous or based on experiences of iteration (as Greimas himself pointed out) (Fig. 2).

This figure describes the itinerary of the entire rhythmic group, drawing a vector, which can be ascending or descending depending on whether the strong tempo of the group is at the beginning or at the end. This is the necessary prerequisite to explain the phenomenon of *iteration* as a constitutive feature of the group itself. It is based on a fiduciary relation between the observer actant (the internal point of view) and the external observer subject: the latter recognises the presence of rhythm only if the first group repeats itself, responding to the simulacrum of the perceived that the enunciator has been able to construct for himself (This is why there is no rhythm except from a third event, which comes after the first and its repetition, which grounds the expectation of the perceiver).[11]

*Fiduciary expectation* is an imaginary movement based on a belief that gives rise to a perceptual *necessity*, a semiotic constraint superimposed on the continuous succession of the process. The pleasure that accompanies the recognition of a rhythm, the pleasure of conjunction of an expecting subject derives from the satisfaction of this necessity.

## PASSION AND COGNITION

Rhythm represents a *cognitive movement combined with a passionate investment*. Narratively, it is the construction of the continuous through iteration, thus through the projection of the discontinuous into duration, by reciprocal concatenation of autonomous groups. Its iterative movement introduces into the textual unfolding a *memory* of the states of conjunction (the *events*) and disjunction (the pauses, the intervals), which is articulated on

---

11 See also Marco Jacquemet's works on rhythm and its perspective qualification (1983, 1991).

a perspective will: just as the absence of the object of desire describes a tensive parabola (see Fig. 1) until there is the acquisition, so the fiduciary lack, located after the terminative phase of the group (corresponding to the interval), calls the repetition of the group itself, without which the tension that can be said to be *predictive* (circular drive) would disappear.

But the question we will try to answer remains the same: why are certain pregnances fixed in particular saliences that produce rhythmic effects?

According to Greimas and Courtés (1978/1983, p. 166), 'Iterativeness is the reproduction along the syntagmatic axis of identical comparable entities which are situated at the same level of analysis'. If these entities can be defined as rhythmic groups, the phenomenon of rhythmic iteration can be considered necessary as a first form of narrativity, an evenemential difference that results in discontinuity projected onto the durationality of the continuous time of expectation.

Due to the fact that it is based on a fiduciary contract, iteration represents a type of *prospective narrativity*. Once the first group has been produced (where certain recurrences, the phases, are recognisable and measurable), it is necessary, for configuration to take place, that the proposed pattern is repeated, thus resulting in the construction of a regular pattern, consistent with the predictability of the observer actant. The interval between one group and the other will therefore be the neutral period necessary for the final equilibrium of the configuration. Expectation, on which the rhythmic configuration is built, is strongly binding: it is the simulacrum that anticipates (i.e. presupposes) the succession in order to be able to set up what is simultaneous (or almost simultaneous: the group).

There is no configuration without repetition of two groups (there is no second group if the first does not appear). Their relation is one of mutual presupposition. In addition, the second group must be repeated in an identical manner as the first (identically to the first): the iteration is based on a *mnestic matrix* – a kind of competence inscribed in the first group at the time of its appearance – which follows (may follow) a constant performance in the expected return of the identical, allowing for the confirmation of the external subject who expects it.

## EQUILIBRIUM

Let us take the diagram sketched above to illustrate what the fundamental notion of *rhythmic equilibrium* consists of and what is the role of the aspectual investment, which has only been touched upon so far.

The standard pattern of a rhythmic group begins, as already mentioned, with a *silence*. This silence describes a state of lack and/or desire, and can be discursive in different ways: typographical space, description prior to the incidence of a fact, enumeration... This silence creates a tension that the first event will soon fill: there is a transition between the duration of the tension of expectation and the punctuality of the inchoative event. But after this event, the tension, initially diminished by the resulting conjunction and satisfaction, will increase again (durative phase) with what has taken place, until the second event will renew a punctual aspect. The moment of transition from one state to the other corresponds to the durational situation (expectation-tension) on which the rhythmic group stands.

Like all tensive relations, the one governing the group is an oriented relation (see Fig. 3): this allows us to advance in our theorisation and to account for two elementary models of the rhythmic structure of the group.

The strong tempo can therefore be placed at the beginning of the group (descending rhythm) or at the end (rising, ascending rhythm). The events/pulses may have the same or different intensity, be stronger or weaker.

We have not predicted patterns where this strong tempo would be in the centre, and for several reasons. On the one hand, the group can definitely only consist of two pulses, one of which would easily be stronger than the other; on the other hand, the proposals of psychologists (Fraisse, 1963) and phoneticians (Halliday, 1985) agree, with experimental data to back them up, that the strong tempo is always located on the first or last phase and never in the centre; finally, and this is a fundamental reason, a model in which the strong tempo would be located in the centre would represent nothing more than the coupling of an ascending and descending rhythm. In any case, everything depends on the segmentation criterion adopted: although a strong tempo may, theoretically, be in the middle of a group of three, nothing would prevent an artificial segmentation from splitting the group in two, and producing two groups of two. We can therefore affirm that there is, in each case, a directionality of the energy impulse within the group and an intensification/disintensification of the perspective projection. The tensive expectation, which we saw earlier, is coupled with a distensive expectation, and both must be met, or the *rhythmic equilibrium* will be destabilised.

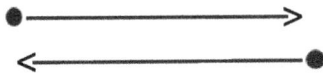

**Fig. 3. Oriented Relationship.**

## PREGNANCE (PRÄGNANZ) AND SALIENCE

In his 'semiotic' theory of biological regulation, as Jean Petitot[12] reminds us, René Thom introduces the concept of *prégnance*, distinguishing between two types of *salient* forms: those that are configurations that stand out against an amorphous background, and those that are *biologically significant*, whose recognition is necessary and psychologically charged. The latter are the *pregnant forms*.

Pregnance is invested in salience in a similar way to the investment of value by a subject on an object, and the conversion of pregnance into catastrophes described by Thom[13] is comparable to the conversion of fundamental semantics into actantial syntax. Now, rhythm brings double homologation into play:

– at the semio-narrative level
  /disjunction/vs/conjunction/
  /actualised/vs/realised/

– at the discursive level
  /tension/vs/distension/
  /expectation/vs/satisfaction/.[14]

While, at the semio-narrative level, actualisation corresponds to a state of phonic concentration that opposes extension and follows the realisation of the rhythmic event (the pulse), on the discursive level, rhythm is above all a *figurative* fact that precedes in abstraction the figurative typical of the alternation of silence (or pause, or graphic/typographical void).[15]

These oppositions, iterated, structure the movement of rhythm. The tension/distension categorisation is perceived on the surface; but it is in the *quo* instances of fundamental semantics that we must seek the measure and the foundations of its pregnance. The resulting interest is that of a definition capable of taking on the essential characteristics of the rhythmic phenomenon:

(1) rhythm as a salient form on which *pregnance* is invested;

(2) the topological organisation of rhythm;

(3) the binary and periodic dynamics of the typical rhythm pattern.

---

12 See the entry 'Prégnance' [Pregnance] in the dictionary by Greimas and Courtés (1986, p. 174).
13 See, inter alia, Thom (1988, 1990).
14 These oppositions are the same as those Greimas identified as pertinent to the semiotic description of the configuration of fiduciary expectation, Greimas (1983/1987).
15 In this regard, see the article by Zilberberg (1989).

The problem that arises, therefore, is how to conceive the discretisation of the substance of the content through the introduction of an immanent discontinuity, independent of the plane of expression (cf. Petitot, 1985/2004, 1992).

## RHYTHM AS SALIENCE

The tension/distension categorisation is a privileged surface opposition for the investment of pregnance. However, *rhythm is a salience par excellence*, liable to become pregnance. Certain pregnances *may preferentially be invested* on tension/distension oppositions, and a rhythmic structure would in this sense have a privileged function for anchoring pregnances on saliences.

The pregnances invested in rhythmic systems pursue a stability of the perceptual grid, almost a biological regulation of the symbolic activity. The recognition of certain forms as *stronger* and therefore more stable, continuous, implies their preferential choice, their 'saisie'.

Hence, the system of pregnances must also be considered as a competence, a biological memory, a set of rules aimed at balancing the perceptual situation.

*A rhythm is a salience*. It is therefore both a morphology and an archetype, an elementary form of temporal syntax. As a temporal syntax, rhythm descends from the figurative, but at the same time is objectively privileged at the moment of the investment of pregnances. In this respect, it is also related to fundamental semantics. Rhythm then takes on the configuration of a syntactic morphology, of a *geometric system of discontinuities* that appears within a structurally unstable logos L, describing a closed space K that can be qualified as a *catastrophic set*. The elementary rhythmic catastrophe is a catastrophe of bifurcation, identifiable with a *ripple*: on a cyclic time that would turn without rhythm, the rhythmic bifurcation rupture is opened, introducing temporal discontinuity.

## RHYTHM AS OSCILLATOR

Rhythm can also be defined as a marked oscillator: *there is rhythm when a cycle is marked*.

Now, the pregnant rhythm-form falls into a category of universals that is by no means abstract, but belongs to the group of *universals of experience*, primitives that concern the content even before it is put into language.

Robert Martin (1983), who provided one of the most comprehensive definitions, writes that the universals of experience come rather from the idea that certain data of the world, physical, physiological, anthropo-cultural, exert such a strong constraint on human life that it is unthinkable that they leave no trace in language, and these traces have every opportunity to be universals. The confrontation of the body, the positions it can take (standing, laying, sitting), the movements it allows, the physiological sensations of fatigue, hunger, thirst, perception through hearing, sight, touch, the experience of heaviness, the orientation of the body and the organisation of space resulting from this; contact with liquids or solids; the alternation of day and night, ageing and death are there, among many others, as inescapable experiences, unlikely to be without repercussion in language (1983, p. 38). This long series of biological rhythms (spontaneous, provoked, induced, acquired), of motor rhythms, of sucking and chewing, of swaying, all the satisfaction that man derives from the simple fact of synchronisation according to an exogenous or endogenous time, is necessarily reproduced in the systems of representation that are proper to him, starting with the image and language. Rhythm is there as a morphological pattern that is imprinted in perception, giving rise to a kind of *sensory memory that predisposes one to appreciate the representations that conform to it*.

Going further and assuming that man, as a sensitive subject, is endowed with a rhythmic competence that is confirmed as the elementary (elastic) morphology of his perceptual system, we also see that this system necessarily interacts with the forms of the world, another system (another morphology) that has investment zones, the pregnances, and more Gestalt zones, the *saliences*. These two concepts have been essential in explaining what is meant by rhythmic *preferential sensitivity*, and what it has in common with the question of equilibrium.

## TRANSCODING: THE NOTION OF ISOMORPHISM

Beyond the various possible manifestations, it appears that there is a *presence of rhythm across all forms of expression*. But in our hypothesis, rhythm may occupy a far more strategic position, identifying it as the *matrix of the transcoding process*,[16] i.e. the transfer from one language system to another.

---

[16] 'We may define transcoding as the operation (or set of operations) by which an element or a meaningful set is transposed from one code into another, from one language into another language' (Greimas & Courtés, 1978/1983, p. 348).

Metz, in *Language and cinema* (1971/1974, pp. 216–217), makes an important distinction regarding the different types of *codical interferences* between languages:

(1) The localised interference, partial and does not concern systematic study;

(2) The codical interference without sensorial transposition, where the same code can be found in several arts or language systems;

(3) The codical interference accompanied by sensorial transposition, where distinct, more or less *isomorphic*, codes are manifested in a different language system: and here is where the coding transposition takes place, since 'a certain logic of what is perceptible, even if it remains the same as logic, is no longer the logic of the same perceptible thing'.

To verify the role of rhythm in any transcoding process, it is therefore necessary to first define the notion of *isomorphism* within a semiotic system.

Isomorphism is an identity of form that can be recognised between different planes (of expression, content), and between units of different sizes. In the third case of codical transposition, we can say with Metz that it is not a question of total isomorphism (otherwise it would be the second case), but of an equivalence between the texts established on the internal network, on the economy of form of the content on a purely relational level. The units, of variable size, of the form of expression (which differ according to the type of texts concerned) will therefore correlate with the constant units of the form of content. It can therefore be said that different figurative categories are homologated to a single content category.

In transcoding, a *semi-symbolic system*[17] such as rhythm necessarily plays a key role, as it can intervene in the coordination between categories of expression and categories of content.

As an *operator of transcoding*, guaranteeing the maintenance of the invariance of the plastic characteristics of a text, rhythm is confirmed at the centre of the individual's cognitive modelling processes.[18]

---

17 A semi-symbolic system is a signifying system characterised by the correlation between categories, and not between units, of the plane of expression and the plane of content (cf. Hjelmslev 1943/1961). By homologating underlying categories of figurativeness to axiological/semio-narrative categories, rhythm can be recognised as a semi-symbolic system (cf. also the entry 'Semi-symbolic', Greimas & Courtés, 1986, pp. 203–206).

18 We elaborate on this essential aspect of defining rhythm in the chapter of this thesis on the conceptual structure.

## RHYTHM AS DEVICE

One of the essential questions of the relation between a text and its description or interpretation (T' or T') certainly remains that of *spatio-temporal* correspondence. If T' relates to T' as its semantic presupposition, its syntactic configuration implies a necessary mediation between two spatio-temporal configurations: one, paradigmatic and synchronic, the other syntagmatic and diachronic, a *regulated deformation* produced by transcoding.[19]

Following Gérard Genette, Seymour Chatman (1978) notes, in the category of temporal relation of *order*, the possibility that the story and the discourse have the same succession, or that there are anachronic sequences (analexis or prolexis) that may have a different scope and breadth, or even that it is an anachrony where there is no chronological relation between the story and the discourse. *Duration* concerns the relation between the time in which the work is received and the time in which the events of the story unfold, with five possibilities: summary, ellipsis, scene, extension and pause. The iterative forms, which interest us most, are derived from the third Genettian category, *frequency*: here, the relation can be singular, singular-multiplicative, repetitive, iterative. Time functions, inevitably, in the spatial and simultaneously temporal sense, as a *device*, a structure that organises the economy of T", and interpretation or narration are irrelevant.

In order to account for the qualitative and positional montage to which the perceptual fact is subjected at the moment when, linguistically named, it is circumscribed and translated into writing, and for the montage, also qualitative and positional, by which, on the other hand, the scriptural text (action plus description) is *translated*, for example, into a performance text (or filmic text), it seems essential to use a double grid, *spatial and temporal*,

> *This intuition of a homogeneous medium, and intuition peculiar to man, enables us to externalize our concepts in relation to one another, reveals to us the objectivity of things.*
> (Bergson, 1904/2001, p. 236)

Rhythm, which structures the perceived as a *form of movement*, manages the relation of the signifying form between the texts involved in the transcoding operation as a distribution of signifiers according to certain periodic

---

19 The notion of transcoding is vast, so let us specify the different ways of understanding it: from a theme/content to an expression; from an object to its metalanguage; from one genre to another genre; in the sense understood by Ricœur (1983/1990), from a prefigured time to a refigured time.

and repetitive patterns – in each case differential – in correspondence with one another.

Finally, let us return to Benveniste (1966/1971, p. 287), to whom we owe the meticulous lexicological analysis of the Greek word mentioned at the beginning of this chapter; it should be emphasised that, already in this text, rhythm takes on an absolutely plastic connotation, where from the 'spatial configuration defined by the distinctive arrangement and proportion of the elements, we arrive at "rhythm", a configuration of movements organized in time'.

## RHYTHM: A STRATEGY

It is obvious that, even if one of our objectives is to verify the definition of rhythm as a rule of invariance (*connection code*) between text and text – those rules, therefore, which are placed at the level of the form of the content (semio-narrative syntax) – we do not forget the importance of rhythm in the form of expression: but since the subject matter of expression changes according to the different texts, it is not conceivable to think of relating *units*, but *categories*. These categories are of a *plastic* nature: eidetic[20] and topological even before being temporal. Their task is to maintain the connection between the form of expression and the form of content. Their relationship, as we have anticipated, is semi-symbolic.

And this is where the *autonomy of the rhythmic device* as such begins, as a mechanism capable of constructing a poetic object, thanks to this second type of semiotisation that does not descend from the connotative but from the Jakobsonian poetic function (projection of the paradigmatic onto the syntagmatic, cf. Jakobson, 1963).

The *connection*, whose code we are seeking, finds its principle here. This is the question common to planar (two-dimensional) semiotics: to individualise the signifying constraints *imposed on the manifestation of signification* (Greimas & Courtés, 1978/1983, p. 282) and – we would add – to verify the degree of isomorphism between two different planes of expression that presuppose an equal distribution of content.

This is why research on rhythm cannot be limited to configuring the structure of the rhythmic device as a perceptual experience (perception of

---

20 It must be made clear that 'eidetic' is here opposed to 'morphemic', since the eidetic descends from the intelligible and not from the form as such.

discontinuity) or as a mode of categorisation (recognition of symmetries and repetitions). We must also attempt to configure it as a generative procedure, as a *constraint* to which corresponds, at the level of narrative syntax, an expectation (and, even more profoundly, a *pre-conceptual competence*). We therefore propose to understand rhythm as a *narrative strategy*, capable of programming a configuration of expectation that will be realised at the discursive level, renewed by continuous iterations (enunciative marks corresponding to as many states of dissatisfaction:/wanting-to-be-conjoined/). A semio-narrative structure is such because it brings into play a subject, an object of value and an anti-subject: the search for value thus gives rise to two rhythmically symmetrical and opposite narrative paths, which are then discursive (taken over by the instance of the enunciation that figurativises them). Any narrative unfolding whose discursivisation presents a subdivision into rhythmic groups can indeed be conceived as a *rhythmic strategy*, if it is true that 'Narrative discourse appears then to be a locus of the different forms of human communication, produced from tension, and of returns to equilibrium' (ibid., p. 205).

Certain thymic (pulsional) and aspectual overdeterminations (putting functions into process) intervene in the semio-narrative, managed by a pre-lexical identity of the subject that we can call *rhythmic competence.*

This means that the subject actant is informed by the intervention of temporal components (ordered and not necessarily isochronous alternation of inchoative, durability, terminative and punctuality sèmes).

On the other hand, but not at a secondary level, rhythm can also be defined as a *discursive strategy* that descends from the instance of enunciation and implies important pragmatic reflections. It is precisely here, still on the tension/distension categorical axis, that we see the simple figures organised in a *rhythmic configuration* (discursive semantics), or that we observe the accent/pause scansion through the play of verbal tenses, that of syntactic collocation, of focus, of frequency and order, of clutching/unclutching (*embrayage/débrayage*) and of internal and external referentialisation (discursive syntax).

# 4

# THE RHYTHMIC GESTALT: CONSTRAINTS AND CONSEQUENCES

Across the different disciplinary domains we explored, we encountered an identical structure, iterative and consistent in its 'group' configuration, present in the discourse without, however, belonging exclusively to it.

Our need to fully understand the rhythmic phenomenon leads us to further investigate these two aspects – independence and formal unity – which make rhythm analogous to a Gestalt.

The aim of this chapter is therefore to provide a critical presentation of the core concepts of the Psychology of Form, from Ehrenfels' seminal article (1890) to more recent developments, where Gestalt theory is re-discussed and integrated into the approaches to perception and interpretation.

In this way, we hope to put into contest – and validate – our initial hypothesis *regarding the pregnance of rhythmic Gestalt.*

We will articulate our argument in three points:

(1) A concise presentation of the origins of the debate, within psychology and philosophy, from which Gestalt theory derives; we will address some laws of form, the field theory and the dynamic conception of space, the isomorphic models and the reflections on memory, intelligence and action;

(2) A sharp critique of these concepts, mainly centred on Piaget's (1967) comment against perceptual schematism and for a revision of the Gestaltist understanding of balance in the sense of self-regulation;

(3) Gestalt re-elaborations and the application of the *rhythmic operator*; we will discuss the concepts of pregnance and salience, and of equilibrium and field according to René Thom; the concept of 'asemantic' pregnance according to Jean Petitot (1985/2004), Ray Jackendoff's (1983)

'preference rules', the distinction between local and global categorisation, the 'grouping judgement', the concepts of ground and figure according to Douglas Hofstadter (1979), and finally, the convergence of the Gestalt representation and the 'basic level structure' in the categorisation proposed by George Lakoff (1989).

Our intention is to show not only the density of concepts relating to the Psychology of Form but also their extreme vitality, the real interest they always hold, even for seemingly distant disciplines such as semiotics.

We are also particularly interested in the fact that Gestalt theory constitutes the essential reference for proceeding to a deeper exploration of a central notion in our conception of rhythm, that is, *regulation*.

## THE ORIGINS OF THE DEBATE

The Theory of Form appeared in Germany in the early 1900s, proposing the notions of *form* and *structure* at the crossroads between the physical and mental worlds. As Petitot (1985/2004) observes, the concept of structure was the subject of reflection both for the generation of the founders of Gestalt theory (Stumpf, Meinong, Ehrenfels) and for the next generation, that of the Berlin School (Wertheimer, Köhler, Koffka; cf. Smith, 1988) well before the structuralism of the 1950s and 1960s.

At the heart of the Theory of Form is the notion that perceptions are like structures, organic complexes that translate the system of punctual sensations into a 'real transformation of the state of consciousness' (Petitot, 1985/2004, p. 35).

The debate on the notion of form and its qualities opened with an 1890 essay by von Ehrenfels, *Gestaltqualitäten* (Smith, 1988, pp. 82–117). In this essay, Ehrenfels introduces the fundamental distinction between *sensation and form qualities* (Gestaltqualitäten) through the example of the perception of a melody: in the melody, sensation qualities correspond to the stimuli caused by the sound vibrations, while form qualities, as Paul Guillaume[1] writes, are a perception of the relations between the vibrations.

It would therefore seem that there are two perceptual stages, two levels of complexity, corresponding to two different psychological objects for the same phenomenon. For Ehrenfels, there is a duality between sensation and representation, between each of the perceived elements of the melody, the notes and

---

1 Cf. Guillaume, *La psychologie de la forme* [Psychology of Form] (1979, p. 18).

sounds, and the melody as a whole, conceived as a relational structure. Beyond an artificial dismemberment, the separation between these two qualities seems indeed arduous, where notes and sounds necessarily vary according to the subjective sensitivity of the perceiver, who simultaneously absorbs and transforms them into a complex form.

Originating as a reaction to nineteenth century psychology, Gestalt theory endeavours to demonstrate that it is possible to move beyond the purely analytical and passive stage of the description of sensation and perception of the sensible to the active, constructed and structured stage of the *formal articulation of the perceived. Psychic facts are considered as forms*, i.e. as elaborations of stimuli, which remain objective beyond the individual (subjective) constitution of the representation. They are *transposable forms*, i.e. they have certain constants that allow the unity of their organisation to be recognised despite two different representational appearances. It is Ehrenfels again who provides the example of the re-memorisation/recollection/remembrance of a melody, a recall that is clearly different from the original melody– but to which it nevertheless relates.

## WEAK AND STRONG FORMS

This notion of *transposability*, or rather, of isomorphism, allows us to advance the hypothesis according to which a real difference can no longer be established between organic forms and physical forms, since the analysis of psychic forms must bring out analogies with physical forms, and vice versa. For Gestaltists, forms are divided into *weak* and *strong* forms. The *strong form* is that of each element that makes up a structure, while the *weak form* is the formal value of the bond that unites the different components. Between weak and strong forms, there is an *equilibrium in the changing dynamics*, the final result of which, however, does not change. This means that the general tendency of changes of state always tends towards the acquisition of *stability*.

The notion of form is conceived on three levels, *physical, physiological* and *psychological*, which can be homologated through isomorphism, thus establishing a structural agreement that is fundamental to understanding the complex nature of the object. Based on these indications, it is evident that for each physical object *there are several theoretically possible psychic forms*, legitimate actualisations of an identical virtuality.

However, Gestalt theory is keen to point out that these are the privileged forms of grouping and selection that makes it possible to envisage 'the best possible form': they must be *regular, simple* and *symmetrical*. But there are also certain fundamental conditions in the organisation of (especially visual) forms, which we now enumerate (cf. David Katz & Lazarsfeld, 1955, pp. 25 ff.):

– The law of proximity;

– The law of similarity;

– The law of closed forms;

– The law of 'good' contour, or common destiny;

– The law of common movement;

– The law of experience.

It still remains to mention the most important law, that of *pregnance*, which is present in all individuals regardless of the influence of environment and experience. This fundamental concept was first enunciated by Max Wertheimer (1912): he introduced the principle of the structural coherence of *good form*, i.e. the tendency of the essential characteristics of the object towards the greatest possible regularity.

If these first laws of form give an idea of how Gestaltists consider as possible and effective the explanation of the system of constraints that accounts for the perceptual outcome at the three different levels (physical, physiological, psychical), it is however necessary to emphasise the principle underlying these laws. It lies, in our view, in the attempt to explain the necessity and mode of *difference* as a criterion for the construction of the phenomenological object. The perceived, whatever the sensory order to which it belongs, inevitably presents itself in this case as a *figure* (let us recall the strong dependence of visual perception on Gestalt terminology), in contrastive relation to a certain *(back)ground*.

## GROUND AND FIGURE

The *figure* and the *ground* are therefore interdependent and interchangeable: privileging one means giving the other the function of a reference field, and vice versa. Now, the problem of the relation between ground and figure is a question of the *internal organisation/distribution of the perceptual field*. But there is an apparently more important or at least more general distinction, which is that of the relation between the subject and the external world: it is a question of the organisation of the *total field*. It is a bi-polar organisation that permanently crosses human life, but whose limits – according to the Gestaltists – are far from being stable. According to Guillaume, in the field of perception and representation, the self forms an organisation that is both merely subordinate, and more or less referred back to the ego (1979, p. 129).

Subject and object thus appear as two ways of sharing the total field of perception; they are the result of the distribution of stimuli. But there is another fundamental point that concerns the attitude of the subject within his environment, that is the non-separation between perception and action, which leads directly to the *dynamic conception of space*, inaugurated by Wertheimer's (1912) article on stroboscopic motion, where the sensation of perceiving movement is provoked by objects that are not in motion.

The impression of movement can thus be caused by one or more sensory modalities, leading to the conclusion that the dynamic perceptual space is one and can be filled by objects of different sensory modalities (Koffka, 1935).

As far as the fundamental concepts of Gestalt theory are concerned, we have so far stated mainly four points:

a. Phenomenological objects are contours endowed with a form;

b. These forms are dynamic and depend on the laws of grouping;

c. The constant nature of the forms themselves is subject to the distribution of the total perceptual field;

d. According to the principle of isomorphism, phenomenal and behavioural things stand in an analogous relation to real things and have similar consequences on psychic 'things'.

## ACTION, MEMORY, LEARNING

A second aspect of the Theory of Form concerns the behaviour of the subject in three different areas of human experience: action, memory and learning. On this subject, Guillaume explains that perception prepares and regulates action and it is intended to make possible the adaptation of the living being to its environment. The aspects of reality that it reveals are those that affect practical life; on the other hand, it develops above all with the movements of the receptor organs, so that it is both cause and effect of the act (1979, p. 125).

The aim of the Theory of Form is to avoid a conception of action as reflex, specifically channelled: motor reactions must rather be considered as the result of tensions produced in the cerebral field by stimulations of different magnitudes.

The movement developed serves first of all to reduce those tensions and re-establish the energy balance; sensitivity and motor action appear closely linked by a function of self-regulation that translates the dynamism of the reaction into the dynamism of perceptual space. Each change in reaction corresponds to a re-organisation of the objects which present themselves under a new aspect; the new reaction introduces new tensions which the new acts try to resolve. It is also in this direction that experts address three central nodes of human psychic processing: memory, intelligence, expression.

The problem of *memory* is analysed in two stages, that of association and that of reproduction: with regard to the first stage, Gestaltists reject the idea that association can be produced by the simple spatio-temporal contiguity of two objects; this only favours the organisation of form on condition that the subject has a pre-existing will to organise – the qualities of the elements of a set, in order to associate spontaneously, depending on their position, must be particularly strong and frequent.

With regard to the second stage (recognition/reproduction), rather than the recognition of the image of the object, it is the recognition of the original interpretation of this same object that is fundamental to enable its reproduction. It is therefore not the individual elements that leave traces, but their formal structure as a whole. Reproduction does not necessarily depend on habitus or other types of continuous bonds between subject and object, but on the overall configuration that may or may not concatenate the tension that enables 'perseverance' (cf. Köhler, 1929).

In the same sense, regarding *intelligence*, Gestaltists lean towards a dynamic conception of conceptual structure: intelligence is any absolutely new *adaptation* of the primary basic formal organisation, any attempt to resolve accidental tensions into changes of structure. On the one hand, there is the resistance of forms, on the other, the capacity for re-organisation: that is the reason for the inequality of intellectual capacities.

It is impossible to separate intelligence from sensory functions; between intelligence and perception there is a relation of isomorphism, based on the same organic, organised and dynamic comparison. Guillaume goes on to say that it is impossible to study mental functions without taking social life into account, without addressing the problem of human-to-human relations (p. 188).

And that is why the Theory of Form is ultimately concerned with the question of human expression. The idea is always that of the homogeneity, or rather the analogical relation between physical and psychic facts, considered in their appearance. The deep emotional dynamics, which respond to *biophysical rhythms*, are thus manifested for Gestaltists in external behaviour, which obeys the same movement.

## PERCEPTUAL SCHEMATISM AND SELF-REGULATED EQUILIBRIUM

To the fundamental problem of defining perception – as an act of thought or constructive movement that specifies the role of cognitive structures in their interaction with the organic world and the constraints of a semiotics of the natural world – Gestalt responds with the *theory of isomorphism*, the intersection of the psychic, the physical and the organic. It is the most controversial and interesting aspect of the Theory of Form: Jean Piaget discussed it subtly in *Biology and Knowledge* (1967/1971) and in *The Psychology of Intelligence* (1947/2001).

For Gestaltists, the conformity between the organic world and the perceptual world is given by the 'laws of organisation', which are considered equal at all levels, diachronic and invariable. In *The Psychology of Intelligence*, Piaget remarks that: '[...] elements perceived in the same field are immediately bound together in complex structures in accordance with precise laws, i.e. the "laws of organisation"' (pp. 56–57).

Gestalt, for Piaget, can thus solve the problem of the genesis of form, but without going too far into the associationist theories of nineteenth century empiricism. Associations are replaced by the molecular idea of global structure; but the fate of the 'passivity of automatic mechanisms' (p. 64), which manages the transpositions from the physical to the psychic and vice versa, remains obscure.

But the Theory of Form, while admitting the existence of ontogeny, only deals with adult perception and, in so doing, ends up considering all perceptual and evolutionary stages as equivalent.

In *Biology and Knowledge* (1967/1971), Piaget criticises in particular the non-dynamism of the notion of equilibrium among Gestaltists. Far from being thought of as the progressive acquisition of a balance of forces, equilibrium is reduced to a simple equivalence, without history or development. However, it is unthinkable that conceptual structures are immovable, as Gestalts are given once and for all. Piaget proposes to rethink the encounter with the object as a selective and relational activity, where the identified equilibrium is the end product of the subject itself and not a cast of the physical field.

## REGULATION

This bring us back to the central notion of *regulation*: the subject compensates for external provocations by adapting his or her own perceptual activity to patterns of action and, at the same time, to changes in the environment, *perceptual Gestalts are never* acquired and certainly even less independent of cognitive structures, and *reciprocal interaction and regulation are constant.*

Piaget, as we can see, does not reject Gestalt proposals; he simply attempts to make their formulations less categorical and deterministic, to introduce a principle of graduality and reversibility, or even evolution, in the relations between the physical, physiological and psychic worlds.

We find it useful to consider again the relation between two structures, the first physical-organic and the second cognitive-perceptual, and to consider the latter as an *isomorphism with partial analogy*, which allows us to read transcoding as a transformation process capable of leading from one of the comparison terms to the other. The perceptual grasping can then be proposed as a transformation of the evenemential, which preserves the information while keeping the relations between the elements unchanged (although the elements, in terms of expression, change); but also, and above all, it can be envisaged as an operation that enriches information, orders and realises it, thus constituting what descends from interpretation (cf. Hofstadter, 1979).

The relation of partial analogy should not be understood as hierarchical, from the physical or physiological to the cognitive, but as an *internal* (Object-Object, Subject-Subject) or *external* (Subject-Object) *self-regulating* relation.

Piaget (1942, 1967/1971) distinguishes three levels of complexity of *regulatory mechanisms*: morphogenetic, structural and functional. The most complex is the functional level, where the logic of grouping resides, which allows two systems to be linked together (remember that the Gestaltists, with their proposal of the 'laws of good form', had raised the same problem).

The intermediate level is that of the anchoring conditions of the groupings, of the structure, which indicates the changes tolerated in the definition of the two systems conceived as isomorphic. But the level of self-regulation that is of fundamental interest to us is the primary, or morphogenetic, level: it is precisely at this level that it is possible to reflect on the elementary mechanisms of perception in order to postulate the existence of a *primary periodicity*, and we shall now see in what sense.

## EQUILIBRIUM, REGULATION AND RHYTHM

In his 1942 article on the fundamental structures of psychic life, Piaget wrote that elementary action consists of movements that are repeated under similar circumstances. This is, in our opinion, the common denominator, the indispensable characteristic of an isomorphic model, but also the most essential definition of a concept as ambiguous as *rhythm*.

Gestalt theory has well understood the need to emphasise the importance of rhythm at the organic level, as a natural ability to group isolated elements together in order to achieve a primary configuration of the perceptible. In other words, we can say that rhythm overdetermines the perceptual situation in the sense of self-regulation (although Gestaltists have moved towards a more determinist approach).

It seems appropriate, then, to put forward a proposal for the integration of Gestalt principles. Based on the hypothesis that rhythm manages the elementary mechanisms of perception located at the morphogenetic (or organic) level, the regulatory activity of the structure envisaged by Gestalt and the dynamic nature manifested in the subject's attempt to resolve the object's internal tensions are in reality *periodic equilibrating actions*. They alternate with antagonistic phases, 'equilibration' for Gestaltists, 'regulation' in Piaget's revisited proposal: *rhythm can in every respect be considered as a control procedure*, both of perception and of action.

The psycholinguist Jean Caron (1983), for his part, transferred the dominant functions of the regulatory act – orientation and compensation – to the discursive setting. This is identified as a 'field'. It is from this field that the unfolding of the interaction, through the different regulations, tends to build an organic whole that evolves towards a state of equilibrium.

The idea common to the notion of control/equilibrium/adjustment seems to be that this series of operations represents a kind of strategy, both at deep and surface levels, intended to favour the anchoring of the subject of perception and its harmonious reception of the phenomenal situation, on the basis of a disposition/compensation/adjustment of its relation with the object that tends towards the *optimisation* of the relation.

## THE NECESSARY ORDER

There is, as Ernst Gombrich writes in *The Sense of Order* (1979), a need for regularity that seems to be universal and that *predisposes favourably* to certain regular, even regularised situations: 'Needless to say the perception of meaning can never be switched off, but for the understanding of decoration we have initially to concern ourselves with the perception of order' (p. 2).

The idea that Gombrich develops in his argument, that the need for regulation is essential and universal, is so broadly defined that the author recognises rhythm (defined as an *aptitude for regularity*, constrained by interaction) as the common denominator of variants, 'the continued aspiration of the visual arts, both static or kinetic, to rival the miracle of music' (ibid., p. 289).

Any rhythmic perception is a *source of pleasure*, because rhythm provides the most natural place to inscribe a perception in a 'regular' pattern, 'since the idea of rhythm depends on the memory of a time interval, and our ability to hold this memory in anticipation of the next sound' (p. 288).

It is clear that, in this hypothesis, rhythm increasingly resembles a higher law among the 'laws of good form' and the configuration of the pregnant structure capable, through natural pathways, of directing the perceptual grouping towards an aesthetic attitude (positive recognition of regularity echoing the latent need for order).

## PREGNANCE, RHYTHM AND REGULATION

In a 1973 article, *De l'icône au symbole* [From Icon to Symbol], René Thom defines perception as the modification of a competent dynamic under the sensory impact of external reality (p. 88). He also adds that the system of competences (i.e. retina, visual cortex, etc.) regains the pristine condition necessary for a total and permanent competence at every moment – and yet certain plasticity exists because perceived sensations are stored in the memory (ibid.). We can clearly see here Thom's reading of the Gestaltist theory of perception, which derives precisely from the idea of field equilibrium, albeit developed in a dynamic, interactive and not purely 'conservative' sense. The structure of perception is an unstable morphology that reacts to any change in the sensory field, at the cost of maintaining a 'noise' in the interactive exchange.

However, according to Thom, in addition to Gestalt forms there are *salient* forms, *pregnant* forms and in particular *biologically relevant* forms which he defines as the ability of a form to evoke other biologically important forms and thus to be easily recognised and classified in the (perceptual or semantic) universe of the subject (p. 93).

These are forms with functional efficacy, a criterion that would explain the preferential sensitivity of the perceptual organism towards them. *Pregnance has a regulatory meaning* for the organism (predation, sexuality, etc.), while saliences are configured as contours (form/background), sudden stimuli that represent intersecting nodes of the perceptual field.[2]

In this context, stability is preserved beyond partial changes but with a reversal of positions, since the pregnances are carried entirely by the Subject of perception, and it is the external field that is appropriated by the Subject. The Subject seduces the Object, but this Object is imposed by its affective pregnance. Rhythm, which Thom calls a 'rhythmic cell', is a continuous generating field, a spatio-temporal support structure that allows the quantification of perception and prepares the encounter/intersection between physical and affective pregnances.

Jean Petitot also takes up the concept of pregnance, but with an even different stance. If Thom follows the evolution of biological pregnances into semantic pregnances in human beings, for Petitot the theory of pregnances is close to Freudian metapsychology, which can be interpreted in this context as a theory of the way in which the symbolic relays the pregnance and, thus charged with the unconscious, interferes with the cognitive (1985/2004, original ed. p. 219).

Unrepresentable because it is invested by an unconscious content, therefore 'asemantic', this type of pregnance, which exists in the fundamental semantics, of a thymic nature, must be kept distinct from the substance of the content, which already contains (according to Hjelmslev's indications) a principle of form. Rather, this form has the task of 'symbolising' pregnances, of articulating them in perceptual differences. This is the theory of emergence, of the 'morphogenesis' of meaning.

---

2 In another essay, *La danse comme sémiurgie* (1990) [Dance as Semiurgy], Thom chooses dance as an aesthetic form to make his understanding of gestaltism explicit. He distinguishes two levels in dance, the global level of the ballet, which reflects the form according to which one dances, and the perceptual level of the dancer, which reflects the sound form. The organism of the dancer encompasses a state of availability to the sound form that is the desire for the appropriation of the gestalt form; the sound form can thus be qualified as the *induced field* and the dancer's affective range as the *inducing field*. Then what is dance? A field of struggling pregnances, depending on the dancer's position X and the instant T, a field synchronous with the sound form, which is in turn the maintaining form that ensures the unity of the field variations.

## REVERSIBILITY AND ISOMORPHISM

The American cognitivist Douglas Hofstadter borrows the concepts of figure and ground from Gestalt theory in his major work *Gödel, Escher, Bach: An Eternal Golden Braid* (1979). Hofstadter poses the problem of the reversibility of the two partitions of the field, emphasising the double valence of the contour, which can privilege either positive or negative space as a figure. In this type of figures, we always recognise something; a second type of figures, known as *currents*, has no possibility of being recognised as negative space.

With regard to recurrent forms, Hofstadter offers an analogy with the musical contrast between melody and accompaniment, or between high and low tempo: two distinct musical tendencies whose importance can be reversed.

Hofstadter also takes up the notion of isomorphism from Gestalt theory, but he invests it with other responsibilities: isomorphism is no longer just a principle of homologation between physical, physiological and psychic structures, but becomes in this case 'the information preserving transformation' (p. 49) between two corresponding structures. It is the perception of isomorphism that creates meanings in the human soul, at two levels: the *lower* one, of correspondence between the parts of two structures, between symbols and words in a logical system, which is equivalent to interpretation; the other, the *higher* one, which corresponds, still in a logical system, to the interpreted propositions and theorems, and thus defines the level of meta-interpretation.

## LAWS OF PERCEPTUAL ORGANISATION

George Lakoff, in *Women, Fire and Dangerous Things* (1989), proposes a relevance of Gestalt theory at the basic level of categorisation, which includes the cognitively fundamental categories. For the author, they are 'functionally and epistemologically primary' and reflect Gestalt perceptual criteria of image formation, motor movement, knowledge organisation, *prior* to cognitive processing (learning, recognition, memory) and *prior* to linguistic expression (p. 13). It is the level of interaction with the natural world, the perceptual stage that allows difference to be established, before moving on to more elaborate stages of experience.

At this level, Lakoff considers the experience structured but in a pre-conceptual manner, where discontinuities are traced in the continuum of possibilities as whole blocks that are imposed by their pregnance. It is an exclusively physical experience, halfway to conceptual elaboration, and which should be read as a proposed mediation between objectivism and realism.

For his part, Jackendoff (1983, pp. 128–160) reinterprets Wertheimer's laws of perceptual organisation and thus formulates his 'preference rules', fundamental constraints, or 'grouping judgement'. Wertheimer enumerated the laws of similarity and proximity: similar and proximate elements tend to be grouped into configurations, to be extracted from the continuum (whatever sensory order they belong to); according to Jackendoff, these two laws are necessary but not sufficient conditions for the formation of the 'grouping judgement', which can be defined as the essential act of discretisation/categorisation of the world.

The author attempts to go beyond Wertheimer's initial reflections on grouping and to demonstrate that there is a structure of grouping, capable of being imposed. This is how he arrived at the formulation of 'grouping preference rules', notably in his research on music with Fred Lerdhal, about which he writes: 'We chose the term "preference rule" because these rules establish not inflexible decisions about structure, but relative preferences among a number of logically possible analyses' (1983, p. 132).

The hypothesis is that the perception is constituted by projection onto the signifying surface of a structure constructed by taking into account all applicable 'preference rules'. These can be classified as local (proximity, similarity, duration) or global (equality, parallelism, coherence).

## THE IMPORTANCE OF 'PREFERENCE RULES'

For Jackendoff, preference rules are an attempt to explain the reasons for the inevitability of a certain type of perceptual grouping: but if the author seems to be able to demonstrate the existence of a certain pregnance in discretisation, preference rules could in our opinion also be used to establish the likely emergence of more complex judgements, such as the value judgements. It is then clear that our position is very close to Gombrich's (1979) reading of Gestalt theory, where he explains the favourable attitude – pleasure – triggered by the presence of grouping factors coinciding with man's desire for order. It is, ultimately, the *encounter of two structures*, that of the Object and that of the Subject, and the 'preference rules' provide the possible reasons for the successful or failed encounter between the two.

In conclusion, we can say that the legacy of the Psychology of Form brings the following contributions to our *definition of rhythm*:

(1) Starting from the principle of isomorphism, it is possible to reconcile the effect of meaning with the phenomenological object that constitutes its pretext, according to certain projective or emergent modes;

(2) If the laws of good form are understood as constraints, or laws of preference, it is possible to establish some anchoring criteria for both description and judgement;

(3) Anchoring criteria lead to categorisation, where recognition takes places in a pre-linguistic and pre-conceptual domain;

(4) The discretisation of the material continuum is thus not necessarily subject to naming, but lexematic research can reveal the deep mechanisms of a self-regulating and dynamic perceptual articulation that pre-exists it.

# 5

# THE COGNITIVE PRAGMATICS OF RHYTHM

Rhythm represents a fundamental *morphological operator*, linked to the pregnant areas of perception, stable Gestalts and their pathemic consequences; but it also represents a *pragmatic device*, a signifying practice that can be recognised in the discursive manifestation, at the crossroads of a theory of representation and a theory of reception.

In both cases, rhythm seems to fulfil the characteristics of an elementary and virtual grammar of pathemic-cognitive distribution, which can only be considered realised when applied to the figurative density of a specific semiotics.

While the rhythmic phenomenon can be certainly considered as a *form of aspectualised discourse*, it must also be qualified in two other ways:

– That of a 'perceptual regulator' active in the determination of meaning;

– That of a 'pragmatic device', which opens up a renewed competence of discourse.

Rhythm would thus be an abstract scheme of perception that operates on syntax. Our hypothesis defines this 'device' as a fundamental structure of psychic life, likely to intervene in the primary processes of cognitive regulation. What rhythm powerfully brings into play is the *dynamics of the relation between perception and action*.

## FROM AUTOPOIESIS TO PRAGMATICS

We are therefore led to verify the *conditions of plausibility of an isomorphism between rhythm, cognitive structures and regulatory mechanisms*; which is to say that the fundamental isomorphism between biological and cognitive structures, present in the rhythmic conceptual structure, would be the fulfilment of a programme of organisation and regulation. It confers on the discursive manifestation an additional value of influence on the activity of the receiver (at all levels: thymic, cognitive and pragmatic).

If we accept this proposition, it follows that it is the play of positive and negative conditioning, typical of rhythm, which produces the semiotic constraints that affect affective and intellectual processes. This is a 'bridge' structure, which sets up a model with a biological basis and a semiotic vocation.

In order to resolve the apparent ambiguity of the dual organic and discursive nature of rhythm, in the first chapter we discussed, the autopoietic theory of Maturana and Varela, authors of an important reflection (cf. Maturana & Varela, 1980, 1987; but also Varela, Thompson & Rosch, 1991) on the conflict between biological and linguistic reason, as well as on the epistemological relevance of the self-regulation model.

We have thus been able to verify that the essence of an autopoietic system is the capacity to use to its advantage the random environmental inputs surrounding it, modifying its own organisation in order to maintain a 'constant' structure. This type of evolutionary process can therefore be seen as a development of the Piagetian intuition of 'perceptive regulations', Gestalten, compositions resulting from a dynamic equilibrium of compensation and conservation. Mauro Ceruti (1989) writes in this regard that this is where the intimate relation between life and cognition finds its roots. The heart of the intimate problem of life is cognition. The core of the problem of life and cognition is co-evolution, the creative dance of conservation and change, of invariance and novelty, of closure and openness. The relationship between subject and object, between knowledge and reality, the learning relationship, is redefined as a relationship of co-emergence, of co-evolution, a dance, precisely, that creates, that 'brings forth' a world, where the required condition is the efficacy of action, which ensures the continuous conservation of the system involved (pp. 190–191).

Like systems theory and autopoietic systems, Gestalt theory has helped us not only to illustrate the transition from organic to cognitive structures but also to situate the configuration in a 'field dynamic'. In connection with these still very general remarks on autopoietic and Gestalt systems, we would like to emphasise the following points:

(1) Autopoiesis is the manifestation of a cognitive field, which means that it is a structure that has taken on the *dynamism of its organisation* and the cognitive potential of its transformations;

(2) Autopoietic systems interact with each other, which means that they construct *behavioural adaptations* that represent communicative interactions, capable of constituting, as Maturana and Varela write, 'a domain of [...] consensual conducts' (1980, p. 120);

(3) The represented interaction produces an observer, an actant that controls the cognitive sphere, justifying its relativity and containing its transformations.

Defining rhythm in terms of an autopoietic system is for us a way of emphasising once again the transcodic vitality, the transversality, the neutrality of a grid, which is 'empty' but exerts a strong constraining function, as a structured system which is nevertheless integrated into very different discursive manifestations.

However, it seems possible to identify here some elements that allow us to go further: *the presuppositions of a pragmatics based on cognitive evolution*, accounting for the relation, in a perceiving being, between the environment and the regulating structure.

In *Mind, Code and Context* (1989, p. XVII), Thomas Givòn writes:

> *Pragmatics is an approach to description, to information processing, thus to the construction, interpretation and communication of experience. At its core lies the notion of context, and the axiom that reality and/or experience are not absolute fixed entities, but rather frame-dependent, contingent upon the observer's perspective.*

If we find here the identical conditions we mentioned earlier, as the hallmarks of a self-regulating system – reaction to an environment, interactive evolution, regulation by an observer – we can also recognise some of the relevant features of a rhythmic structure.

## TOWARDS COGNITIVE PRAGMATICS

We are convinced that in the complex relation existing between organism, mental structure and behaviour, the pragmatics of rhythm is able to provide an explanation, other than that provided by psychologists, to at least three fundamental phenomena:

(1) The positive judgement of value (consensus) that generally follows the recognition of a rhythm;

(2) The physical dynamism that a rhythm is always likely to stimulate in its recipient;

(3) The presupposition of isotopy, i.e. interaction, that a rhythmic configuration develops.

These three points, or 'rhythm effects', refer – in our opinion – to a central question: *how does subjectivity regulate the emergence of meaning by formulating an enunciative field* with illocutionary value and contextual modulations?

We have defined rhythm as a 'conceptual structure'. This is to say that we favour, on all manifestations and at all levels where rhythm can be perceived, its assimilation to a *cognitive filter that mediates between perception and discursive action*. The pragmatic relevance of rhythm is therefore understood here, above all, in the cognitive sense, and consequently not in a strictly linguistic sense. We need to explain this further.

Cognitive pragmatics stems from the effort to identify an integrated interpretive pathway between behaviour and cognition. The idea is that neither concepts nor perceptions alone can form the basis of mental categories: it is only from their integration that a plausible construction of experience can occur.

Any pragmatic approach subjects interpretation to contextualisation. But, in cognitive pragmatics, the purpose of the action involves the mind of the sender as the context of the proposition to be followed. The ground is then identified with the norm on which an information (figure) becomes salient. Concepts and perceptions form a context in their interaction.

> For us, this "pragmatics" of language which has reference to the characteristics of its utilization constitutes one of the aspects of the cognitive dimension; for it concerns in fact the cognitive competence

> *of the communicating subjects, such as it can be recognized (and its simulacrum reconstructed) within the utterance-discourse.*
> *(Greimas and Courtés 1978/1983, p. 241)*

While pragmatics in the Greimasian sense obviously seems much closer to the cognitivist conception of the discipline (cf. Givòn, 1989) than the better-known pragmatics of the American school (based largely on the work of Morris), the definition of rhythm as a *pragmatic, semiotic and cognitive strategy* appeals to a theory of enunciation that also takes into account the *effect of enunciation*, where an enunciation effect is not present in the utterance in the form of morpho-syntactic or semantic-syntactic markers or indicators, but has to be reconstructed or 'discovered' through an interpretive effort (cf. Parret, 1987, p. 113).

## THE ENUNCIATIVE MARKING

We must now trace the markers capable of activating the rhythmic device, which may confirm the assumption that rhythmicity is also a specific 'mode of enunciation'. We know that every theory, whether enunciative or pragmatic, must make use of two parameters that constitute essential reference markers for its analytical capacity: *deicticisation* and *modalisation*.

It is true that it is possible to identify in rhythm the principles of an 'actional' syntax, within the enunciative sphere that enacts the basic constraints of the rhythmic system: *constant numerical distribution/group structure and iteration*. But it is also true that enunciation is the condition that makes any utterance possible, and its rhythmic connotation depends as much on the enunciative marks as on the competence, which we can define as 'passionate', of the subjects involved in the interaction.

There are three well known components of deixis: *space, time and person*. Rhythm introduces into the utterance a series of deictics, which, on the one hand, constructs the progression of transformations of the subject of the utterance and, on the other, the conditions of possibility of a rhythmic 'saisie' on the part of the enunciator.

Jacques Geninasca (1992) who analyses rhythm from an enunciative point of view with regard to three-term serial syntagmas, writes that the euphoria that concludes a rhythmic sequence arises under the combined effect of the proprioceptive feeling of an overabundance of available energy and the sudden revelation of a principle of order and intelligibility, more powerful than that of linear regularities (and their combinatorial variants). The term is not the expected equivalent of a and b, but that of the set they constitute (a, b) (p. 255).

The rhythmic cell is an elementary structure that the deixes allow to recognise, manoeuvring the iterated configuration both in terms of expression and content. Two linked expressions are enough for the rhythmic expectation to take hold, for there to be a lasting tension directed towards the actualisation of a third term. It is in this way that, within the discourse, elements of coherence are placed, points of support that allow a perceptive 'grip' that is both iconic and motivated.

Deictics structure the distribution of meaning as well as the interaction with the recipient, and can consolidate into rhetorical figures (anaphora: the meaning relies several times on the same verbal element; epistrophe: the movement is modified at the beginning to be regularly brought back to the same form; antithesis: the repetition of a syntactic construction that emphasises an opposition of meaning, sometimes accompanied by the repetition of certain words). But deictics can also deal with the return of a word or adjective, an identical/analogous phrase or an identical/analogous grammatical structure.

Marks can certainly be accents or timbres, if we are dealing with a poetic rhythm. They may correspond to the lengthening or shortening of an interval, if we are dealing with a musical or graphic/plastic rhythm. But if it is a more generic verbal rhythm, the rhythm will first of all correspond to the alternation of *embrayage* and *débrayage* procedures. The marks of subjectivity will then be the pronouns (and secondly, the *verb tenses*), whose alternation can give rise to a rhythmic schematisation.

Nor should we forget the pragmatic importance of rhythm that intervenes at the oral level in *paralinguistic, prosodic* and even *gestural terms*.

## A PRAGMATIC STRATEGY

The double possibility of the existence of the rhythmic structure is based on the *competence/constraint* relation. It is then possible to say that rhythm also takes the form of a *pragmatic strategy*. For us, a pragmatic strategy is a *regularity of a competitive nature*, i.e. the condition that allows a structure of order to come into being and produce certain contextual consequences. Parret, in his definition of 'pragmatic strategy',[1] to which we largely adhere, opposes this notion to that of *law, rule* and *generalisation*. A pragmatic strategy – in this sense – has a translinguistic capacity to adjust interaction and a normative capacity, which means that it provides a memory of pregnant structures, ready to be renewed in the discourse. In this respect, in Chapter Five, we recalled that rhythm is a conceptual device of *synchronisation/congruence* between an external 'oscillator' (the discourse) and an internal 'oscillator' (the conceptual structure); when the synchronisation between the one and the other is interrupted, a need for adaptation arises, so that the crisis of confidence caused by the expectation can be resolved in a positive way.

The essential gestures of every enunciative strategy (field organisation, referentialisation, evaluation, anchoring, modalisation and illocutionary scope) are thus charged with dynamic values. This means that the regulation of the discursive situation is inscribed in a configuration of an aspectual nature that aims to maintain a reasonable tension within the discursive articulation and that translates into perceptual manipulation in order to orientate the passionate and cognitive transformations of the subject of perception and, in accordance with its biopsychic constraints, its predispositions to rhythm.

Working on the temporal organisation of perception and action, McKay demonstrated that the rhythmic distribution of a discursive production facilitates perception. There is also, between the rhythms of production and perception, a real interaction (a 'regulation', therefore, as shown by the association of movements, breathing and even speech, as an output with respect to a rhythmic input). Fraisse (1974) had already shown that rhythm produces a motor induction, and that this sensation is accompanied by a feeling of pleasure.

In other words, we can say that rhythmic regulation is above all a temporal interaction, 'compatible' or 'incompatible' (i.e. harmoniously correlated or not with the action of the receiver performing it): this relation between perception and action, between production and reception, is realised in the temporal and periodic coordination of the factors of perceptual stimulation and receptive action. McKay, in *Perception and Action* (1987), calls these coordination nodes 'cognitive clocks' and emphasises their functioning both at a syntactic and semantic level and at a pragmatic level, in the very sense of muscle activation.

---

1 'Strategy', definition 1 = 'an internalised and enhanced regularity that generates the discursive fragment from the context of enunciation' (Parret, 1987, p. 179).

## COMMUNICATIVE CONTRACT AND RHYTHMIC MODALISATION

In the previous analysis, we reaffirmed that the functioning of rhythm would respond to a *strategy*, at the crossroads between cognition (competence) and discourse (performance). The idea is that language can be understood as a *system of regularities*, whose redundancy is emphasised by the presence of rhythm. But the term 'redundancy' – as Bateson (1972) points out – is synonymous with 'structuring' and thus, at least in part, with 'meaning' (p. 420).

In communication, as well as in the universe of natural phenomena, redundancy allows the observer to trace back from the perception of a part of a sequence or configuration to the whole: the principle that governs this type of statement is the consideration that a redundancy always introduces a 'habitus' in the subject of perception that allows the latter to grasp the rules of repetition until it reaches an encoding that will allow its prediction.

We have dealt with these phenomena in detail in the semiotic part of this work. What interests us now is, on the one hand, what Bateson himself states, namely, the relevance of this phenomenon not only for the 'constructed' world but also for the 'natural' world (transversal characteristics of each rhythm), and, on the other hand, the *imprinting* related to this type of grouping that attributes to the conceptual structure certain 'adaptive' configurations, learned in the relationship with the environment. This means, for us, that rhythm derives from a primary conceptual form, i.e. the establishment of an interactive relationship between the subject and the world.

## THE NOTION OF 'HABITUS' ACCORDING TO PEIRCE

This contract, which we can call a 'communicative contract', has an implicit and not necessarily reciprocal nature: it can therefore be either intra-subjective or inter-subjective, and be based on a veridical presupposition. The notion of communicative contract resulting from discursive redundancy and the triadic normativity of rhythm reminds us of the concept of habitus that the American pragmatist Charles Sanders Peirce[2] conceived in his theoretical elaboration.

In Peirce's theory, the sign is the sum of two instances, the 'Representamen' and the 'Immediate Object' (assimilated, respectively, to the expression and content of the sign), which give the percept its first iconic representation: the

---

2 Cf. the article *A Survey of Pragmaticism* (1931).

dyadic relation is thus transformed into a triadic relation when the sign is perceived and becomes a mental representation ('Dynamic Object').

The 'Dynamic Object' is also what Peirce defines as an 'interpretant'. In Peirce's theory, 'interpretants' continue each other in what is called 'unlimited semiosis': the 'final logical interpretant' of an intellectual sign can only correspond to a change of 'habitus'. The 'habitus' provisionally concludes the discussion and thus represents the structuring of a paradigm that the following experience/action may, because it is different, call into question. The evolution of a process thus takes place according to a precise rhythm that establishes its normativity/unstable equilibrium, through a three-stage dynamic that can be repeated ad infinitum.

The repetition of actions accelerates the change of habitus, but iteration is not considered by Peirce to be solely responsible for these transformations: he also mentions surprise, inner effort and conjecture.

## AN INTERNALISED COMPETENCE

The regulating activity of rhythm – whether perceptual or language-related – is constantly structured around a game of adaptation, of constraint, taking shape through the construction of a pragmatic strategy, i.e. an internalised competence mutually recognised by the language community. This is, in our opinion, very precisely comparable to the Peircian habitus, which, as in the case of a rhythmic representation, does not necessarily have to coincide with a mental representation, but can give rise to a physical behaviour/action.

The notion of *constraint* becomes clearer: it may derive from the constitutive elements of the semiotics of the natural world, from linguistic models, or even from the society that practices the language in question; more often than not, it comes from the three 'systems' at once.

However, the communicative contract of which rhythm, through its manipulative power, is one of the driving forces, matches phenomenal occurrences with the linguistic ones. The problem of rhythm is a problem of relation: the observer uses it as a system of coordinates that can order occurrences either successively or concurrently (Culioli, 1990, p. 56).

As an organisation of phenomenal occurrences, rhythm leads back to the 'underlying' structures, which are physically and biologically anchored and belong at the same time to the experiential *imprinting* and learning of the observer; as a grid of linguistic occurrences, rhythm used as a pragmatic strategy proves to be responsible not only for the plastic structuring of the form of expression but also for the semantic value determined by the positional ordering managed by the observer-actant.

If we consider rhythm as an organisational field of a contractual nature – or physical-cultural 'domain' – we can verify the presence of at least one 'attractor' that enables the constitution of the rhythmic group as a point of concentration in the sense that, whatever the correspondence of the sphere considered, the attractor contains it by assimilation or identification (p. 61), and which, in our opinion, allows the existence of actual *rhythm motifs* to be recorded.

What matters, for now, is that rhythm bears witness to a *regulated linguistic activity*, where certain phenomenological and gestalt constraints (proximity, iterativity, similarity) impose on the continuity of phenomenal occurrences a form that translates them into linguistic occurrences. There are certain operations that govern this transition. It is in this sense that one can speak of a close interweaving of the cognitive and the linguistic: every enunciation, every discourse creates, at the same time, a certain image of the relations between 'things' (objects, situations, spheres) and the conditions for reading – in the sense of retrieving – this representation (Vignaux, 1988, p. 166).

## RHYTHMIC MODALISATION

The 'construct' envisaged by any enunciation or discourse must take into account not only the system proper to the chosen language and its constraints but also the *operations that focus on the primary relations of the perceivable.* These are essentially the *predicative relation, thematisation, focalisation and modalisation* (cf. Vignaux, 1988).

At least as far as semantic rhythms are concerned, all these relations can be involved in a rhythmic schematisation. The distribution of predicates, of themes and patterns, of viewpoints that give the discourse its orientation and reading dynamics, is handled by this kind of primary operation. But the one that interests us most is *modalisation*.

By *modalisation* we mean more precisely – within cognitive pragmatics – the attribution of discursive representation by means of certain modal values that manage not only figural time and space (cf. Zilberberg, 1989) but also the relation linking *enunciative subjectivity* to the *cognitive appropriation* thus prepared. These modal values are 'Wanting' and 'Having-to-Know', which intervene in the tensiveness of the rhythmic network in the splicing dynamic, and 'Believing', which ensures the coherence of the rhythmic isotopy, as well as the formation of the triadic group after the realisation of the dyadic relation between an event and its iteration.

*Modalisation* modulates the discourse of the cognitive-linguistic operation and introduces a point of view that reveals the implicit presence of the enunciator, adding a pathemic connotation to the rhythmic pattern. The modal relation is considered in this sense as fundamentally intersubjective, establishing the relation between two actants.

This *double structure covered by modalisation* also allows it to be the operation that best accounts for the *isomorphism* of the *rhythmic pattern* with the dynamics of the narrative tension. For rhythm, the ago-antagonist structure is the basis of the group's composition and the minimal unit of its configuration. The narrative structure is itself an alternation of states of conjunction and disjunction resulting from the fundamental opposition between the subject actant and its anti-subject. The rhythmic group thus implies an alternation between tensions of opposite signs (ascending/descending), which 'dialogue' with each other in an iterative way, until a motif is identified.

This type of discursive structuring has certain pragmatic consequences (as an 'action' on the perceptual grasp), in that it can influence the behaviour of the locutors and, in return, inevitably use the context to ensure the configuration (the laws of proximity and similarity that give rise to the rhythmic 'good form' are laws subject to the influence of the context, of the background against which the figures will take a certain prominence).

The *rhythmic modification*, which intervenes on the different phases of the group's tensive curve, allows a distribution of the pragmatic influence of the 'device' and, in addition, a modulation of the value attributed on a cognitive and thymic level to the elements that make up the recognised path. It implements the conceptual representation scheme of rhythm.

# 6

# RHYTHM AS AN AESTHETIC TACTIC

If rhythm can function as a conceptual structure and as a pragmatic strategy, it is also thanks to its *tactical presence* in the manifested discourse. We are neither referring to perceptual rhythms, nor to rhythms that belong to the macrophysics of the world. What we are interested in here is to see how rhythm acts on the signifier/signified relation of a discourse, what is its place as *tactics of expression* and *tactics of content*. So why introduce this notion of *tactics* that is apparently alien to the discursive realities to which we want to apply it? The answer is simple. Throughout this analysis, we have raised a number of issues concerning rhythm as a syntactic, semantic and finally pragmatic *strategy*. The notion of *strategy* has the particularity of presenting itself as a global competence to manage the eventual situation, whereas *tactics* would decide, as a *local competence*, on the execution of the event itself.

This being said, our aim is to succeed, with this second notion, in solving a problem of linearisation that seems fundamental to us, that of defining a *rhythmic style*, and therefore an aesthetic that can be said to be strongly dependent on the rhythmic configuration, by going into greater depth on syntactic and semantic rhythms.

## SYNTACTIC AND SEMANTIC RHYTHMS

In a very general way, we can say that tactics can be defined as a strategy of position that can coincide with a rhythmic configuration. In any case, it refers to questions of *order*, linear order in the case where the signifier is, for example, natural language. François Rastier (1991, p. 222) writes in this regard that the sensitising effect of rhythms at the neuronal level can be related, with the necessary mediations, to the facilitating effects of semantic recurrences that we call the presumption of isotopy, and in particular of rhythmic recurrences encoded in rhetoric.

We can consider two types of tactics, the tactics of expression and the tactics of content, but both interest us because of the synchronising relation they can produce between internal and external oscillators, between neuronal rhythms and discursive phenomenon: generating a harmonisation followed by a feeling of pleasure/positive value judgement whose generative structure has yet to be linearised. This is what we call *aesthetic tactics*, without excluding any other form of preliminary syntactic, semantic or pragmatic strategy.

This reflection is heavily influenced by Rastier's work on the relations between semantics and cognition, and in particular by the paradigms set out by this same author in his work *Meaning and Textuality* (1989/1997). Rastier distinguishes four semantic components: thematic, dialectical, dialogical and tactical. If the *thematic* component makes explicit the invested contents and their paradigmatic structures, the *dialectic* accounts for intervals and aspectual structures, the *dialogic* is the level of modalities, and the *tactical* 'accounts for the linear organisation of the semantic units' (p. 62).

The *tactics of expression* can – according to Rastier – be situated either at the level of the first or second articulation of natural language:

– At the level of the first articulation, the following are the concern of the tactics of expression: at the sentence level, the order of words in the syntagm, the order of the syntagm and the groups separated by punctuations or pauses; at the transphrastic level, paragraphs, sections and chapters of the written; the sequences and sessions that are part of the oral component;

– At the second level of articulation, prosody and metrics involve diversely the three levels of word, sentence and text (1989/1997, p. 63).

Rastier observed (1989/1997, p. 64):

> *On both planes of language, the position relative to the units is codified by norms that are at the same time part of the functional system of language and of other instances. I do not attempt here to untangle one from the other, as distinguishing them is not necessary for the demonstration, in so far as no text can exist without genre. Moreover, in my analysis I distinguish: a) the position relative to the signifieds; b) the position of the signifiers; and c) phonic, graphic, or semantic investments realized in these positions.*

The relation between position and investment obviously brings into question the continuous interaction between tactics of expression and tactics of content. On the other hand, the topological character of tactical organisation refers to an identical evidence of rhythms, both syntactic and semantic.

The *tactics of content* brings into play the intersections between isotopies, as well as the parallel, alternative or branched character of their appearance. The content rhythms they manage can be in correspondence or counterpoint to the accentual rhythms of the plane of expression.

## VERBAL TACTICS

The rhythmic configuration is the place of all iterations: of number, duration, intensity, pitch, timbre and content. It is these iterations that allow it to be perceived, and make it a possible measure of the continuum.

Let us take the example of the syntactic rhythms of French, a language that the vulgate considers eminently musical, making no distinction between verse and prose. Here we consider rhythm as a very open 'movement', which the verse eventually systematises, giving rise to certain specificities.

We will therefore say, first of all, that the fundamental (prosodic) rhythm of French:

– is rarely syllabic;

– is based on the links provided by the last syllable of lexical entities (or the penultimate one if the vowel of the last syllable is a silent/e/).

There is thus a phonic mark that distinguishes the link, the most stable quality of which is the *length* of the syllable (among other qualities, we distinguish intensity, variation and sound quality). The determination of the links depends on several factors, ranging from the pragmatic intention of the speaker to the influence of the length of the syntactic unit, to which supporting, pathemic or even identifying beats are added. The sound rhythm corresponds to an 'additional' rhythm in relation to the basic rhythm: it is the rhythm of timbre, which can both reinforce and control the basic rhythm.

While *intensity* is mainly linked to differences in textual genre which, in some way, encode it, from the point of view of the form of expression, it serves above all to highlight, also sonically, the word or syntagma. It does not leave any specific formal traces in the written language, where we can essentially distinguish the possibility of placing the beat on the consonant or on the vowel, with an aspectually opposite effect: exhortative in the first case and durative in the second. But it can also be placed in the momentum, thus affecting the first consonant of the word, at the beginning or within the sentence, with very different results, from a semantic and sound point of view.

Rhythmic density is better defined as it traces rhythmic movement back to number, to a calculable proportion in its effects, and in which the Ancients had indicated the origin of the sensation of pleasure and harmony generated by the perception of rhythm.

## THE MEASURE OF PROSODIC UNITS

The numerical relation is primarily between the syllable of the beat and the number of syllables of the momentum, which thus participate in the constitution of the elementary prosodic unit. According to Joseph Pineau (1979), prosodic units of different sizes can be distinguished:

a. The prosodic unit of one syllable: a very rapid movement in which the momentum must rest on the initial consonant or vowel that prepares the beat;

b. The prosodic unit of two syllables: the momentum has time to prepare the beat in a more relaxed manner; the syllable of the beat is in any case longer;

c. The prosodic unit of three syllables: this is theoretically the most balanced unit in terms of the relation between momentum and beat: the syllable of the beat being longer, the two syllables of the momentum can match it (although according to Pineau it is not correct to say that in French 'one long is worth two short');

d. Prosodic units of four or five syllables: the momentum begins to outweigh the beat without creating an effective disproportion yet;

e. More than five syllables: the numerical relation becomes more complex and less controllable, the momentum takes on greater importance and large prosodic units can be broken down into smaller ones that repeat the relation structure we have seen.

The perception of the numerical relations between units makes it possible to distinguish different 'figures' of syntactic rhythm: *concentration, expansion, deceleration, acceleration* (based on the integrity of prosodic units) and *regularity* in identical or varied position. The *semantic significance* of these figures, as well as their intervention in the determination of an idiolectal or gendered style and expectation in the receiver will be analysed later.

## THE RHYTHM OF EXPRESSION

As far as the rhythm of expression is concerned, however, the syntagmatic of the different prosodic units will be immediately recalled. In this regard, Pineau (1979, p. 62) writes that the movement of meaning, which determines the place and intensity of the beats, also determines the inequalities of the rhythmic concatenation. It is by following the same dynamism that this movement creates the relative dissociation produced by the beats in the chain of syllables, and that increases or reduces, in each case, this same dissociation. The inequality of prosodic concatenations is essentially tributary to the different elements of syntactic movement: cohesion of syntagmas, lengths of syntactic units, greater or lesser urgency from the start of the momentum; secondly, this principle is associated with the more or less firm desire to emphasise a word, a syntagma, a logic.

*Legato*, pauses, punctuation, *enjambement* correspond to as many concatenation systems, according to continuous or discontinuous movements and depending on the semantic determination of the text. The fundamental *speed*, which derives in particular from the intensity and thus the spacing between momentum and beat, is of decisive importance in the receiver's perception. The tempo with which this speed is identified is a phenomenon closely linked to rhythmic enunciation, which determines how quickly unmarked syllables are pronounced before arriving at the beat that delimits the prosodic group.

That said, it is clearly impossible to determine reference points for defining tempo, except that a fast tempo is generally accompanied by a lower beat density than a slow tempo.

## THE RHYTHM OF MEANING

We can now consider the *rhythms of meaning*.

Largely responsible for discursive tactics, they are generally derived from hierarchical isotopies. We have seen some of the aspects concerning this type of rhythm in the previous chapter: here we would first like to emphasise that rhythm, whatever type it is, is related to semantic choices/effects. The rhythm of meaning corresponds not only to the partial return of the message but also enriches it, marking the progressive construction of the isotopy. It can intervene on the return of an identical syntagma, or of an identical construction, in correspondence with the identity of meaning. It can:

a. be generated by a continuous succession of similar or identical elements;

b. be generated by repetitions that are linked to a fundamental structure (litany, ramifications, intersections, intermittences);

c. be in discordance (counterpoint, contrast) with the fundamental rhythm;

d. be in association or not with the timbre rhythm.

Pineau (p. 128) adds that it would remain to make a typology of styles according to the interplay of the fundamental rhythm and the rhythm of meaning, according to their intensity, and the levels at which their relevance is situated in relation to the material put into play by the rhythm of meaning. This is an immense and extremely delicate task.

It is not our ambition to accomplish this task exhaustively, but we will instead discuss its aspirational implications and, finally, attempt to define how a *rhythmic style* can be constituted.

## THE RHYTHMIC STYLE

Taking the conception of rhythm as a tactic, we feel it necessary to briefly emphasise a few points related to the *aspectual influence on the cognitive configuration of rhythm.*

We know that in Greimasian semantic theory aspectual categories belong to the discursive level. Here, as an expression of the instance of enunciation, which thus imprints its point of view on the discourse, they bring into play the performance of a cognitive actant (the 'observer') who translates the narrative utterances into a process. The observer categorises textual continuity. He manifests an abstract position subject to the constraints of textualisation. We propose to consider these categories as one of the (most fundamental) components of textual montage, a discursive configuration that establishes a syntagm of viewpoints and produces a spatio-temporal pattern that can fulfil the conditions for the existence of a rhythm.

In other words, this means that on the basis of a minimum grid of oppositions traced on the level of expression, and which implements the realised focalisations, displacements and figurativisations of the observer actant, as well as its spatialisation, actorisation and temporalisation procedures, the analysis will be able to reconstruct, on the level of content, the type of actualised process and the actantial positions involved. The observer-actant, within the aspectual movement that brings cohesion to the rhythmic pattern, changes the status of the utterances (from logical to topological) and plays a fundamental role in the viewer's perception.

Jean Petitot writes about this (1992, p. 179) that aspectuality is one of the devices that enable us to move from a narrative syntax of actants supporting interoceptive values (values are semes, thymically invested, produced by a fundamental semantics) to the exteroceptive (figurative) structures of discursivity and in particular to a randomised actantial syntax with linguistic content. We can therefore attempt to redefine it as a component of the semiotics of the natural world.

Aspect then clearly appears to be the 'tensor' of rhythm, at the interface between the natural world and language. And it takes on the responsibility of being considered as the Gestalt presupposition upstream of the enunciative deictics. All this implies a correspondence between the morpho-dynamic structure and the discursivity that remains to be demonstrated, although the rhythmic manifestations – in their pregnance – seem rather explicit. The fact is, as Petitot writes, that the qualitative structures of the phenomenal world are intrinsically meaningful (p. 183): hence the intention of an objective morphological level that allows for the 'ecological' description of the forms and states of things.

If we agree with this approach, we must also change the definition of the term 'tactics', which finds its focus in the aspectual determination: since it is therefore impossible to describe it as an intentional phenomenon, we should then think of a directionality of the strategic mechanism. This directionality is at the origin of the pregnance of rhythm in regulatory systems. The resulting isomorphism between fundamental and surface semantics, between thymic and discursive, is the basis of its textual effectiveness.

The latter is modulated by a double regulating factor, pathemic and aspectual, intended to measure and distribute certain partial balances to prolong the narrative tension. The rhythmic style – a redundancy that realises a presumption of isotopy – produces an *aesthetic effect of a pathemic nature*, according to the 'classical' Jakobsonian scheme of projection of the paradigmatic onto the syntagmatic.

Rhythm, a profound impulse and describable regularity, emerges here as an essential, or perhaps only more evident, actor in the modalisation of a pathemic isotopy. It introduces, paradoxically, a relation of order, a principle of repetition and alternation which, if it explains, in the semio-pragmatic sense, the relation between enunciation and modalisation, serves the linguistic and cognitive sense as grammatical, verbal and rhetorical regularity, and also as the attribution of spaces, of knowledge, of a universe of existence to linguistically motivated objects.

The definition of a tensive or rhythmic style is thus placed at the interface of the pathemic and the thematic, precisely through *aspectual persistence*.

*A tensive style serves to give body and figure to passion, to make it discursive by provoking a lasting suspension of the observer's modal competence.*

Through rhythm, the tense style, always determined and organised by appearance, distributes redundancies throughout the text as so many 'landmarks' that serve to calibrate and distribute the passionate response and make it recognisable, and which intervene to enable us to identify the 'form of movement', as Benveniste called it. The question of rhythm thus raises some more complex issues, touching on the themes of consensus and value.

## RHYTHMIC TACTICS AS A PASSIONATE REGULATION

In conclusion, we will discuss the role of the *passionate regulation activated* by rhythm in the execution of its tactics. The passion we are talking about is inscribed in the discourse and is not a secondary pole in relation to the concept and the perception: in the same way as the latter, it integrates, it speaks of the world and of the subject's relation with itself and with the 'other'. In this hypothesis, there is no subordination between cognitive and pathemic isotopy: there is perhaps a possible predominance, an inflection of one over the other. Between emotion and passion, for the moment we will only place the fragile threshold of aspectual persistence that characterises passion, the only one to which we will pay attention in this case.

The idea is that, if emotion and passion share the awareness of the lack of the object of value expressed in phoric terms, punctual for the former and durative for the latter, the passionate subject (unlike the emotional subject) carries within him the energetic capital necessary for the translation of the pathemic urgency into figures, entrusting the latter with the saturation of the absence.

Denis Bertrand who, in a 1987 article (p. 11) initiated this path of interpretation, argued that these figures together illustrate, according to specific forms of regulation, the saturation movements through which the modal consistency of the absent object is increased *ad infinitum* (i.e. in reality, up to the threshold of the intelligible).

The passionate path thus overdetermines the figurative path to the point of gradually managing the dichotomy between the cognitive and affective dimensions. But the inscription of the pathemic into the discursive – a procedure for converting deep thymus – takes on a different depth (a different 'dosage', one might say) according to the thematic configuration in which it is inserted, and according to the roles involved in it.

In a redundant situation, it is possible to move on to some textual places where passionate regulation seems less necessary or at least less perceptible and where, through the aspectual control that is proper to it, a distribution of interventions is based on pragmatic effectiveness (think of the intersubjective dynamics of a process).

Here we come to the heart of our reflection: the interpathemical is not a mode of intersubjectivity but an aspectual network that allows intersubjectivity to manifest itself, in both the proprioceptive and the exteroceptive sense, preventing the modal subject from sinking into the improbability of a univocal (only attractive/only repulsive) existence, and unable to represent, albeit in absentia, its own desire/investment of value.

*Passionate regulation is*, in other words, *a minimal syntax* traceable through the analysis of enunciative strategies, of the inscription of subjectivity in the discourse. It can also be considered as the 'expedient' that translates narrative tension into discursive 'frame', ordering the 'modal tumult' (Fontanille, 1989) according to a modulated configuration with an aspectual network that allows, among other things, narrative schematisation.

It is as if, between excess and indifference, which represent the extreme thresholds of the subject's passionate existence, a series of figurative 'supports' were woven that allow the itinerary of passion to be narrated and the irregularity that grounds it (the introduction of the imbalance through which emotion bursts into affective life and its discourse) to be translated into the regulation of passionate persistence. Here are all the prerequisites to formulate the hypothesis of a rhetoric of pathos that provides these figures with a logic, the configuration with a paradigm and the subject with the *frame* to recompose an identification.

In the intersubjective relation (be it intra- or extra-subjective, between a subject and itself or between a subject and an object or a second subject), rhetoric serves to regulate the distance between the actants. Why not think, then, that where passion is a rupture of symmetry, an energetic imbalance that stages otherness by posing a conflictual situation as inevitable, *the exercise of a rhetoric of passion such as rhythmisation provides the principle of a new equilibrium?*

This rhetoric would also allow passion to be traversed, i.e. to be enunciated, in the violence of its very alternation between excess and indifference, and yet to be traced back to a reversibility that allows the pathemic clash to always reverse its extremes, to somehow make it part of a contractual distance. This is what we call passionate regulation, and which corresponds for us to the *fundamental rhythmicity of intersubjective exchange.*

# CONCLUSIONS

The *conceptual rhythmic rules* we have listed constitute, in our opinion, the main results of our journey. Through these, we have been able to detail the status of the rhythmic structure, and the morphological level of the encounter between bodily representation and conceptual syntax.

The conceptual rhythmic rules in fact move the question of rhythm upstream of the debate in the natural and human sciences: indifferent to the modes of its discursive manifestation – which can only influence the type of input that rhythm gives to perception – they allow us to understand rhythm as a *form of information*, certainly not the only one, but one that privileges the synchronisation of experiential and conceptual categorisation, both of which are governed by the gestalt principle of *well-formedness rules* (cf. Jackendoff, 1992).

The marked rhythm-cycle thus provides, in our opinion, a first explanation for the pregnance, the salience of which seems to be universally invested; exteroception and interoception know the proprioceptive filter of bodily rhythms, and its reference to the oscillatory activity within the brain (cf. Gerald M. Edelman, 1992).

Does the language of the mind have a privileged syntax in the rhythmic form of information? This is our hypothesis, which refers, among other things, to the universality of the archetypal actantial ago-antagonist structure in which rhythm participates. The elementary configuration of rhythm, which determines an *alternation* between at least three elements, seems to respond precisely to this actantial dynamic.

## THE DOUBLE ARTICULATION

At the interface between organic and mental life, we have already been led to reflect on an object which, when observed closely, participates in three modes of existence. Rhythm is at the same time:

- a perceptual device, which 'introduces order' into the mass of perception;
- a conceptual configuration, which 'organises the understanding' of the perceived and gives it pregnance where its salience is recognised;
- a phenomenon of perception, a 'mode of manifestation' of the referential universe that influences the characteristics of the projected world.

This *form of phenomenon* straddling two structures, one subjective and the other objective, provides for an internal 'group' articulation that establishes a coherence, a recognisable matrix within what René Thom has called the 'rhythmic cell'; however, it also invests the former with a relation between groups that constitutes a second articulation, giving rise to what has been defined as rhythmic *style*.

That said, what seems even more interesting to us is that this complex configuration respects a *figural* and not a figurative principle, that is to say, it represents only a positional and therefore aspectualised scheme, which can accompany, synchronise with, but also contrast and contradict the figurativeness in which it is embedded.

This is another way of understanding double articulation, which can account for some of the most interesting semiotic developments of rhythm: its *plastic independence*, explained by a physically anchored semi-symbolic functioning, justifies its 'universality', as well as its decisive role in the intelligence of the world (cf. Piaget, 1967); it also brings it very close, if not actually assimilates it, to what Jackendoff (1992) called the 'Tenet of Constancy', i.e. that level of mental representation which decides on the segmentation and shaping of information.

## PASSION AND COGNITION

This opens up one of the most significant aspects that we have encountered in the course of our investigation, and which had, in fact, partly determined its beginnings: what is the link between the cognitive function of rhythm, its natural presence and that attribution which can be linked to pleasure, or at least to the satisfaction of an expectation?

We have attempted to answer this question on several occasions and in many ways throughout this book. But it remains one of the richest avenues for future research, also supported by the publication, not recent (1994) but still extremely significant, of the neurologist Jean-Pierre Changeux, dedicated precisely to explaining the relationship between 'art and pleasure'.

According to Changeux, art exploits the predispositions of our brain to 'create' relationships between reason and pleasure (p. 25), and thus the brain's ability to unify and harmonise the mental representation of the artistic object is a synthesis that passes through the seizure of the rhythm of forms and figures, through the recognition of an aspectual organisation (p. 39).

Precisely for this reason, art is close to the organisation of reasoning and to neuronal architectures.

Pleasure would thus function in a similar way to reason, thanks precisely to this rhythmic and isomorphic synthesis; it would ultimately be a concerted mobilisation of sets of neurons located at several levels of organisation in the brain, from the limbic system to the frontal cortex: an enlarged mental object would realise this harmony of sensuality and reason (p. 46).

## A SEMIOTICS OF THE BODY

Another point to which we would like to return is the very particularity of rhythm among structures, among semiotic and natural phenomena. It is indeed one of the most surprising examples of *embodied action*, i.e. experience that influences cognition and that comes primarily, in the case of humans, from a body endowed with sensory-motor capacities, which in turn are embedded in a biological, psychological and cultural context that merely reiterates, amplifies and echoes those same capacities.

This shows that motor and sensory processes of perception and action are closely related to one another. But also, as Varela, Thompson and Rosch (1991, p. 173) write, that

> *(1) perception consists in perceptually guided action and (2) cognitive structures emerge from the recurrent sensorimotor patterns that enable action to be perceptually guided.*

It is certain, in this perspective, that rhythm participates in the activity of categorisation, and in a categorisation scheme based on experience and bodily representations. It thus clashes with the problem of emergence: we can – and we have tried to do so in the course of this work – conceive of rhythm as morphodynamics, a form of a phenomenon derived from physics, phenomenology and semi-linguistic structures.

## (NOT) TO CONCLUDE

The space of this reflection has certainly not been sufficient to grasp all the implications of a form as 'transversal' as rhythm.

We leave to possible future developments the paths of research that, in our opinion, have been opened up here:

- A deeper exploration of the relation between passion and cognition with regard to rhythm, if it is true that we are endowed with two forms of cognition, one computational and unconscious, the other phenomenological and conscious: rhythmic passionisation would in any case be traceable to a form of cognition;

- The question of the double articulation, which presents the irrefutable difficulty of finding the units of first articulation, rhythmic 'signs';

- The problem of pregnance and its relation to cognitive structures: could we not imagine progressive levels of complexity of pregnance that parallel morphodynamic emergence?

- The relationship of rhythm with energy, with a hypothetical thymic category, which would articulate its thresholds of sensitivity;

- The possibility of establishing a correspondence between a syntactic device (at both discursive and narrative levels) such as rhythm, and a self-regulating scheme;

- The compatibility of an intersubjective dynamic, which could not be denied a rhythmic status, with the cognitive approach we have proposed;

- An investigation of rhythm as a thematic unit, a cohesive strategy that syncretic texts such as theatre and audiovisuals are familiar with;

- And finally, a research on rhythm understood as a figural micro-configuration, which functions in correspondence with the content categories in a semi-symbolic way.

# BIBLIOGRAPHY

Various Authors. (1989). Turbulence [Turbolence]. In *Encyclopedia Universalis*. ed by S. A. France.

Various Authors. (1993). Per una semantica dello stile [For a semantics of style]. *Semio-News*, (pp. 9–10).

Augustine, St. (1960). *The Confessions of Saint Augustine* (Ryan, J. K., Trans.). Crown Publishing Group.

Anderson, J. M. (1971). *The Grammar of Case: Towards a Localistic Theory*. Cambridge University Press.

Aristotle (1992). *The Art of Rhetoric*. Penguin Classics.

Arnheim, R. (1974). *Art and Visual Perception*. University Press of California.

Arom, S. (1992). À la recherche du temps perdu: métrique et rythme en musique [In search of lost time: metrics and rhythm in music]. *Les rythmes*. L'Harmattan.

Bachelard, G. (2013). *The Intuition of the Instant* (Rizo-Patron, E., Trans.). Northwestern University Press. (original work published 1932)

Bachelard, G. (2000). *Dialectic of Duration* (McAllester Jones, M., Trans.). Clinamen Press Ltd. (original work published 1936)

Balazs, B. (1970). *Theory of the Film: Character and Growth of a New Art* (Bone, E., Trans.). Dover Publications. (original work published 1949)

Barbieri, D. (1992). *Tempo, immagine, ritmo e racconto* [*Time, Image, Rhythm and Narrative*]. Doctoral thesis.

Bateson, G. (1972). *Steps to an Ecology of Mind*. Ballantine Books.

Beccaria, G. (1975). *L'autonomia del significante: figure del ritmo e della sintassi. Dante, Pascoli, D'Annunzio* [*The Autonomy of the Signifier: Figures of Rhythm and Syntax. Dante, Pascoli, D'Annunzio*]. Einaudi.

Benveniste, E. (1971). The notion of "Rhythm" in its linguistic expression. In *Problems in General Linguistics* (Meek, M. E., Trans.). University of Miami Press. (original work published 1966)

Bergé, P., Pomeau, Y., & Dubois-Gance, M. (1994). *Des rythmes au chaos* [*From Rhythms to Chaos*]. Odile Jacob.

Bergson, H. (2001). *Time and Free Will: An Essay on the Immediate Data of Consciousness* (Pogson, F. L., Trans.). Dover Publications. (original work published 1904)

Bergson, H. (1999). *Duration and Simultaneity* (Jacobson, L., Trans.). Clinamen Press Ltd. (original work published 1922)

Berrendonner, A. (1981). *Éléments de pragmatique linguistique* [*Elements of Linguistic Pragmatics*]. Editions de Minuit.

Bertrand, D. (1987), Le corps émouvant: l'absence. Propositions pour une sémiotique de l'émotion [The moving body: the absence. Proposals for a semiotics of emotion]. *Versus*, no. 47/48. Bompiani. (pp. 1–13).

Bolinger, D. L. (1970). Relative height. In *Intonation*, ed. by D. Bolinger. Penguin. (pp. 137–153).

Boulez, P., & Thévenin, P. (ed.). (1968). *Notes of an Apprenticeship* (Weinstock, H., Trans.). A. A. Knopf. (original work published 1966)

Bouligand, Y. (1980). *La morphogenèse: de la biologie aux mathématiques* [*Morphogenesis: From Biology to Mathematics*]. Maloine.

Bourassa, L. (1990). Rythme et sens [Rhythm and meaning]. *Protée*, Vol. 18, no. 1. (pp. 29–36).

Brandt, P. A. (1988). *La charpente modale du sens: Pour une sémiolinguistique morphogénétique et dynamique* [*The Modal Framework of Meaning: For a Morphogenetic and Dynamic Semi-Linguistics*]. Aarhus University Press.

Brik, O. (1927). *Ritm i sintaksis* [*Rhythm and Syntax*]. *Théorie de la littérature* (1985), ed. by T. Todorov. Seuil.

Brøndal, V. (1943). *Essais de linguistique générale* [*Essays on General Linguistics*]. Einar Munksgaard.

Bünning, E. (1973). *The Physiological Clock: Circadian Rhythms and Biological Chronometry*. Springer.

Calabrese, O. (1985a). *Il linguaggio dell'arte* [*The Language of Art*]. Bompiani.

Calabrese, O. (1985b). *La macchina della pittura* [*The Painting Machine*]. Laterza.

Canepari, L. (1979). *Introduzione alla fonetica* [*Introduction to Phonetics*]. Einaudi.

Caron, J. (1983). *Les régulations du discours: Psycholinguistique et pragmatique du langage* [*Discourse Regulations: Psycholinguistics and Pragmatics of Language*]. PUF.

Ceccato, S. (1987). *La fabbrica del bello* [*The Beauty Factory*]. Rizzoli.

Ceruti, M. (1989). *La danza che crea* [*The Dance Which Creates*]. Feltrinelli.

Chailley, J. (1979). *La musique grecque antique* [*Ancient Greek Music*]. Les Belles Lettres.

Changeux, J. P. (1994). *Raison et Plaisir* [*Reason and Pleasure*]. Odile Jacob.

Chatman, S. (1978). *Story and Discourse*. Cornell University Press.

Chomsky, N. (1968). *Language and Mind*. Harcourt Brace & World.

Chomsky, N. (1986). *Barriers*. MIT Press.

Clynes, M. (ed.). (1986a). *Music, Mind and Brain*. Plenum Press.

Clynes, M. (1986b). *When Time Is Music. Rhythm in Psychological, Linguistic and Musical Process*, ed. by J. R. Evans, & M. Clynes. Charles C. Thomas Publisher. (pp. 169–224).

Cohen, J. (1966). *Structure du langage poétique* [*Structure of Poetic Language*]. Flammarion.

Coquet, J. C. (1984). *Pour une linguistique de l'énonciation: opérations et transformations* [*For a Linguistics of Enunciation: Operations and Transformations*]. Ophrys.

Culioli, A. (1990). *Operations et representations* [*Operations and Representations*]. Ophrys.

Dalcroze, E. J. (1981). *La musique et nous: notes sur notre double vie* [*Music and Us: Notes on Our Double Life*]. Slatkine.

Delas, D. (1989). Approches du rythme [Approaches to rhythm]. *Cahiers de sémiotique textuelle*, no. 14. Université Paris X.

Delas, D. (1991). Silence et rythme [Silence and rhythm]. *Cahiers de sémiotique textuelle*, no. 21. Université Paris X.

Deleuze, G. (1994). *Difference and Repetition* (Patton, P., Trans.). Columbia University Press. (original work published 1968)

Deleuze, G. (1993). *The Logic of Sense* (Lester, M. & Stivale, C., Trans.). Columbia University Press. (original work published 1969)

Deleuze, G. (1973). Structure. In *Histoire de la philosophie*, ed. by F. Chatalet. Hachette.

Deleuze, G. (2001). *Cinema 1: The Movement Image* (Tomlinson, H. & Habberjam, B., Trans.). Continuum International Publishing Group. (original work published in 1983)

Deleuze, G., & Guattari, F. (1987). *A Thousand Plateaus: Capitalism and Schizophrenia* (Massumi, B., Trans.). University of Minnesota Press. (original work published 1980)

De Michelis, G. (1985). *Introduction*. In the Italian Translation of Maturana and Varela (1980).

Denis, M. (1991). *Image and Cognition* (Denis, M. & Greenbaum, C., Trans.). Harvester Wheatsheaf. (original work published 1989)

Descles, J. P. (1986). *Représentation des connaissances: Archétypes cognitifs et schèmes grammaticaux [Knowledge Representation: Cognitive Archetypes and Grammatical Patterns]*. Actes sémiotiques, VII, no. 69/70. EHESS.

Dorfles, G. (1980). *L'intervallo perduto [The Lost Interval]*. Einaudi.

Dowling, W. J., & Harwood, D. L. (1986). Rhythms and the organisation of time. In *Music and Cognition*. Academic Press.

Eco, U. (1979). *A Theory of Semiotics*. Indiana University Press. (original work published 1975)

Eco, U. (1979). *Lector in Fabula*. Bompiani.

Eco, U. (1983). *The Name of the Rose* (Weaver, W., Trans.). HarperCollins. (original work published 1980)

Edelman, G. M. (1989). *The Remembered Present*. Basic Books.

Edelman, G. M. (1992). *Bright Air, Brilliant Fire: On the Matter of the Mind*. Basic Books.

Eibl-Eibesfeldt, I. (1970). *Ethology, the Biology of Behavior* (Klinghammer, E., Trans.). Holt, Rinehart and Winston. (original work published 1967)

Ejzenstein, S. M. (1958). *Na urokach rezissury S. Ejzensteina*. Iskusstvo.

Ejzestein, S. M. (2010). *Towards a Theory of Montage: Sergei Eisenstein Selected Works*, Vol. 2 (Glenny, M., Trans.). Bloomsbury Publishing. (original work published 1963–1970)

Eliade, M. (1954). *The Myth of the Eternal Return* (Trask, W. R., Trans.). Pantheon Books. (original work published 1949)

Evans, J. R., & Clynes, M. (ed.). (1986). *Rhythm in Psychological Linguistic and Musical Processes*. Charles C. Thomas Press.

Fabbri, P. (1991). Il significante del mondo [The signifier of the world]. *Carte Semiotiche*, no. 7. La Casa Usher.

Fabbri, P. (1992). Pertinence et adéquation [Pertinence and adaptation]. *Nouveaux Actes Sémiotiques*, no. 19. PULIM.

Fabbri, P., & Marrone, G. (ed.). (2002). *Semiotica in Nuce [Semiotics at a Glance], Volume II*. Meltemi.

Fabbri, P., & Pezzini, I. (ed.). (1987). *Affettività e sistemi semiotici: le passioni nel discorso*. Versus, May–December., no. 47/48. Bompiani.

Fodor, J. A. (1982). *Modularity of Mind*. MIT Press.

Fodor, J. A., & Pylyshyn, Z. (1988). Cognitivism and cognitive architecture. *Cognition*, no. 26, (pp. 3–71).

Fonagy, I. (1983). *La vive voix [The Living Voice]*. Payot.

Fontanille, J. (1989). Les passions de l'asthme [The passions of asthma]. *Nouveaux Actes Sémiotiques*, Vol. 1, no. 6. PULIM.

Fontanille, J. (ed.). (1991). *Le discours aspectualisé [Aspecualised Discourse]*. PULIM.

Fontanille, J. (ed.). (1992). *La quantité et ses modulations qualitatives [Quantity and Its Qualitative Modulations]*. PULIM.

Fontanille, J. (ed.). (1995). *Sémiotique du visible: Des mondes de lumière [Semiotics of the Visible: Worlds of Light]*. PUF.

Fraisse, P. (1963). *The Psychology of Time* (Leith, J., Trans.). Harper & Row. (original work published 1957)

Fraisse, P. (1974). *Psychologie du rythme [The Psychology of Rhythm]*. PUF.

Fraisse, P., Halberg, F., Lejeune, H., Michon, A., Montangero, J., Nuttin, J., & Richelle, M. (1979). *Du temps biologique au temps psychologique [From Biological to Psychological Time]*. PUF.

Freud, S. (1953). *A General Introduction to Psychoanalysis* (Riviere, J., Trans.). Pocket Books. (original work published 1915–1917, 1932)

Guaquelin, M. (1978). *Cosmic Influences on Human Behavior* (Clemow, J. E., Trans.). ASI Publishers. (original work published 1973)

Genette, G. (1982). *Figures of Literary Discourse* (Sheridan, A., Trans.). Columbia University Press. (original work published 1972)

Genette, G. (1988). *Narrative Discourse Revisited* (Lewin, J. E., Trans.). Cornell University Press. (original work published 1983)

Geninasca, J. (1992). L'énonciation et le nombre: series textuelles, cohérence discursive et rythme [The enunciation and the Number: textual series, discoursive coherence and rhythm]. In *La quantité et ses modulation qualitatives*, ed. by J. Fontanille. PULIM.

Givon, T. (1989). *Mind, Code and Context*. Lawrence Erlbaum Associates Publishers.

Gombrich, E. H. (1979). *The Sense of Order*. Phaidon Press Ltd.

Greimas, A. J. (1968). *Pour une sémiotique du monde naturel* [*For a Semiotics of the Natural World*]. Langages.

Greimas, A. J. (ed.). (1972). *Essais de sémiotique poétique* [*Essays in Poetic Semiotics*]. Larousse.

Greimas, A. J. (1987). *On Meaning: Selected Writings in Semiotic Theory* (Perron, P. J. & Collins, F. H., Trans.). University of Minnesota. (original work published 1983)

Greimas, A. J. (1987). *De l'imperfection* [*On Imperfection*]. Fanlac.

Greimas, A. J., & Courtés, J. (1983). *Semiotics and Language: An Analytical Dictionary* (Christ, L., Patte, D., James, L., McMahon, E., Phillips, G., Rengstorf, M., Trans.). Indiana University Press. (original work published 1978)

Greimas, A. J., & Courtés, J. (1986). *Sémiotique, Dictionnaire raisonné de la théorie du langage II* [*Semiotics and Language: An Analytical Dictionary II*]. Hachette.

Greimas, A. J., & Fontanille, J. (1992). *The Semiotics of Passion: From States of Affairs to States of Feelings* (Perron, P., Trans.). University of Minnesota Press. (original work published 1991)

Grossberg, S. (ed.). (1987). *The Adaptive Brain*. Elsevier Science.

Group μ. (1977). *Rhétorique de la poésie: Lecture linéaire, lecture tabulaire* [*A Rhetoric of Poetry: Linear Reading, Tabular Reading*]. PUF.

Guillaume, G. (1929). *Temps et verbe* [*Tense and Verb*]. Champion.

Guillaume, G. (1979). *La psychologie de la forme* [*The Psychology of Form*]. Flammarion.

Halliday, M. A. K. (1985). Intonation et rythme [Intonation and rhythm]. *Documents*, Vol. VII, (p. 61).

Heiddeger, M. (1996). *Being and Time: A Translation of Sein und Zeit* (Stambaugh, J., Trans.). State University of New York Press. (original work published 1927)

Hjelmslev, L. (1961). *Prolegomena to a Theory of Language* (Whitfield, F. J., Trans.). The University of California. (original work published 1943)

Hofstadter, D. (1979). *Gödel, Escher, Bach: An Eternal Golden Braid*. Basic Books.

Honzl, J. (1940). *Dynamics of the sign in the Theatre*. Seminal essay.

Husserl, E. (1983). *Ideas Pertaining to a Pure Phenomenology and to a Phenomenological Philosophy* (Kersten, F., Trans.). Kluwer Academic Publishers. (original work published 1900)

Husserl, E. (1991). *On the Phenomenology of the Consciousness of Internal Time* (Brough, J. B., Trans.). Kluwer Academic Publishers. (original work published 1928)

Issacharoff, M. (1989). *Discourse as Performance*. Stanford University Press. (original work published 1985)

Jackendoff, R. (1983). *Semantics and Cognition*. MIT Press.

Jackendoff, R. (1987). *Consciousness and the Computational Mind*. MIT Press.

Jackendoff, R. (1990). *Semantic Structures*. MIT Press.

Jackendoff, R. (1992). *Languages of the Mind*. MIT Press.

Jacquement, M. (1983). *Matériel pour une définition du rythme* [*Material for a Definition of Rhythm*]. Le rythme. Colloque d'Albi.

Jacquement, M. (1991). Autour de la petite phrase de Vinteuil: lecture sémiotique d'Un amour de Swann. *Noveaux Actes Sémiotiques*, no. 15–16. PULIM.

Jakobson, R., & Halle, M. (1956). *Fundamentals of Language*. Mouton.

Jakobson, R. (1963). *Essays de linguistique générale*. Ed. de Minuit.

Jakobson, R. (1987). *Language in Literature*, ed. by K. Pomorska, & S. Rudy. Belknap Press.

Jakobson, R. (1981). *Six Lectures on Sound and Meaning* (Mepham, J., Trans.). MIT Press. (original work published 1976)

Jakobson, R., & Waugh, L. (1979). *The Sound Shape of Language*. Indiana University Press.

Johnson, M. (1987). *The Body in the Mind*. Chicago University Press.

Johnson Laird, P. (1983). *Mental Models*. Cambridge University Press.

Jousse, M. (1974). *L'anthropologie du geste* [*The Anthropology of Gesture*]. Gallimard.

Kandinsky, V. (1979). *Point and Line to Plane* (Rebay, H., Trans.). Dover Publications. (original work published 1926)

Kanisza, G. (1980). *Grammatica del vedere* [*Grammar of Sight: Essays on Perception and Gestalt*]. Il Mulino.

Kant, E. (1890). *Critique of Pure Reason* (Meiklejohn, J. M., Trans.). George Bell and Sons. (original work published 1781)

Kant, E. (1892). *Critique of Judgement* (Bernard, J. H., Trans.). Macmillan and Co. (original work published 1790)

Katz, D. (1985). *Introduction à la psychologie de la forme* [*Introduction to the Psychology of Form*]. Rivière.

Katz, D. (1950). *Gestalt Psychology: Its Nature and Significance* (Tyson, R., Trans.). The Ronald Press Company. (original work published 1948)

Katz, E., & Lazarsfeld, P. F. (1955). *Personal Influence: The Part Played by People in the Flow of Mass Communications*. Free Press.

Katz, J., & Fodor, J. A. (1964). *The Structure of Language*. Prentice Hall.

Keane, T. (1991). Figurativité et perception [Figurativeness and perception]. *Nouveaux Actes Sémiotiques*. PULIM.

Kerbrat-Orecchioni, C. (1980). *L'énonciation de la subjectivité dans le langage* [*The Enunciation of Subjectivity in Language*]. Presses Universitaires de Lyon.

Klein, M. (1984). *The Psycho-Analysis of Children* (Strachey, A., Trans.). Free Press. (original work published 1932)

Koch, H. C. (1782–1793). *Versuch einer Anleitung zur Composition [Attempt at a Guide to Composition]*. Harcourt Brace & World.

Koffka, K. (1935). *Principles of Gestalt Psychology*. Routledge and Kegan Paul.

Kohler, W. (1929). *Gestalt Psychology*. Liverlight.

Kovecses, Z. (1989). *Emotion Concepts*. Springer Verlag.

Kristeva, J. (1984). *Revolution in Poetic Language* (Waller, M., Trans.). Columbia University Press. (original work published 1974)

Kristeva, J. (1976). Contraintes rythmiques et langage poétique [Rhythmic constraints and poetic language]. In *Analyse du discours*, ed. by P. Leon, & F. Mitterrand.

Lakoff, G. (1989). *Women, Fire and Dangerous Things*. University of Chicago Press.

Lakoff, G., & Johnson, M. (1980). *Metaphors We Live By*. Chicago University Press.

Landowski, E. (2005). *Les interactions risquées [Risky Interactions]*. Pulim.

Langacker, R. W. (1987). *Foundations of Cognitive Grammar*. Stanford University Press.

Larthomas, P. (1980). *Le langage dramatique: Sa nature, ses procédés [Dramatic Language: Its Nature and Its Processes]*. PUF.

Lerdahl, F., & Jackendoff, R. (1983). *A Generative Theory of Tonal Music*. MIT Press.

Leroi-Gourhan, A. (1993). *Gesture and Speech* (Berger, A. B., Trans.). MIT Press. (original work published 1964–1965)

Lévi-Strauss, C. (1970). *The Raw and the Cooked* (Weightman, J. & Weightman, D., Trans.). Harper & Row Publishers Inc. (original work published 1964)

Lofts, B. (1970). *Animal Photoperiodism*. Edward Arnold Publishers Ltd.

McKay, D. G. (1987). *The Organization of Perception and Action*. Springer Verlag.

Magli, P., & Pozzato, M. P. (1985). *Prefazione. La grammatica narrativa di A. J. Greimas* [Preface. The Narrative Grammar of A. J. Greimas]. In the Italian Translation of Greimas (1983).

Marr, D. (1979). *Vision*. Freeman and Co.

Martin, R. (1983). *Pour une logique du sens* [For a Logic of Meaning]. PUF.

Maturana, H., & Varela, F. J. (1980). *Autopoiesis and Cognition: The Realisation of the Living*. Springer.

Maturana, H., & Varela, F. J. (1987). *The Tree of Knowledge: The Biological Roots of Human Understanding*. New Science Library.

Meinong, A. (1965). *Philosophenbriefe aus des wissenschaftlichen Korrespondenz von A. Meinong mit F. Brentano* [Letters to Philosophers from the Scientific Correspondence between A. Meinong and F. Brentano]. Akademische Druck-u. Verlag.

Merleau-Ponty, M. (1962). *Phenomenology of Perception* (Smith, C., Trans.). Routledge & Kegan Paul. (original work published 1945)

Meschonnic, H. (1982). *Critique du rythme* [The Critique of Rhythm]. Verdier.

Meschonnic, H. (1983). *Le rythme* [Rhythm]. PUF.

Metz, C. (1974). *Film Language: A Semiotics of the Cinema* (Taylor, M., Trans.). Oxford University Press. (original work published 1968/1972)

Metz, C. (1974). *Language and Cinema* (Umiker-Sebeok, D. J., Trans.). De Gruyter. (original work published 1971)

Metz, C. (1977). *Essais sémiotiques* [Semiotic Essays]. Klincksieck.

Meyer, L. B. (1989). *Style and Music*. University of Pennsylvania Press.

Miller, G., & Johnson-Laird, P. N. (1976). *Language and Perception*. The Belknap Press.

Millet, B., & Manachere, G. (1982). *Introduction à l'étude des rythmes biologiques* [Introduction to the Study of Biological Rhythms]. Vuibert.

Mitry, J. (1997). *The Aesthetics and Psychology of the Cinema* (King, C., Trans.). Indiana University Press. (original work published 1990)

Morazé, C. (1986). *Les Origines Sacrées des Sciences Modernes* [The Sacred Origins of Modern Science]. Fayard.

Mounier-Kuhn, P., Lafon, J-C. (May 1969). Les Rythmes. *Postgraduate Medical Journal*, Vol. 45, no. 523, (p. 346). https://doi.org/10.1136/pgmj.45.523.346 (original work published 1968)

Mounir, A. (1989). *La perception des variations relatives des qualités musicales du son* [The Perception of Relative Variations in the Musical Qualities of Sound]. EHESS.

Mukarovsky, J. (1970). *Aesthetic Function, Norm and Value as Social Facts* (Suino, M. E., Trans.). Department of Slavic Languages and Literature, University of Michigan. (original work published 1966)

Nappi, F. M. (1985). *Tempo e significazione ritmica nel film* [Time and Rhythmic Signification in Film]. Pellegrini.

Nattiez, J. J. (1990). *Music and Discourse: Towards a Semiology of Music* (Abbate, C., Trans.). Princeton University Press. (original work published 1978)

Oullet, P. (1992). Signification et Sensation [Meaning and Sensation]. *Nouveaux Actes Sémiotiques*, no. 20. PULIM.

Parret, H. (1987). *Prolégomènes à la théorie de l'énonciation* [Prolegomena to the Theory of Enunciation]. Peter Lang Verlag.

Pavis, P. (1998). *Dictionary of the Theatre: Terms, Concepts, and Analysis* (Shantz, C., Trans.). University of Toronto Press. (original work published 1987)

Peirce, C. S. (1931). *A Survey of Pragmaticism. Collected Papers, 1931–1935.* The Belknap Press.

Petitot, J. (1979). Hypothèse localiste et théorie des catastrophes [Localist hypothesis and catastrophe theory]. Note sur le débat [Note on the debate]. *TLAT*, (pp. 516–524).

Petitot, J. (1983). *Pas même un ange: Le problème de l'émergence du descriptible hors de l'indescriptible* [Not Even an Angel: The Problem of the Emergence of the Describable from the Indescribable]. In I. Prigogine (1988).

Petitot, J. (2004). *Morphogenesis of Meaning* (Manjali, F., Trans.). Peter Lang Pub. Inc. (original work published 1985)

Petitot, J. (1986). *Prégnance* [Pregnance]. In A. J. Greimas and J. Courtés (1978 &1986).

Petitot, J. (1989). Hypothèse localiste, modèles morphodynamiques et théories cognitives [Localist hypothesis, morphodynamic models and cognitive theories]. *Semiotiac*, no. 77. Mouton De Gruyter.

Petitot, J. (1992). *Physique du sens* [*Physics of Meaning*]. Editions du CNRS.

Piaget, J. (1942). Les trois structures fondamentales de la vie psychique: rythme, régulation et groupement [The three fundamental structures of psychic life: rhythm, regulation and grouping]. *Revue Suisse de Psychologie*, no. 1.

Piaget, J. (1969). *The Child's Conception of Time* (Pomerans, A. J., Trans.). Basic Books. (original work published 1946)

Piaget, J. (2001). *The Psychology of Intelligence* (Berlyne, D. E. & Piercy, M., Trans.). Routledge. (original work published 1947)

Piaget, J. (1971). *Biology and Knowledge: An Essay on the Relations between Organic Regulations and Cognitive Processes* (Walsh, B., Trans.). University of Chicago Press. (original work published 1967)

Piaget, J. (1971). *Structuralism* (Maschler, C., Trans.). Harper & Row. (original work published 1968)

Piaget, J. (1972). *The Principles of Genetic Epistemology* (Mays, W., Trans.). Routledge and K. Paul. (original work published 1970)

Piattelli Palmarini, M. (ed.) (1979). *Théories du langage, théories de l'apprentissage: Le débat entre Chomsky et Piaget* [*Theories of Language, Theories of Learning: The Debate between Chomsky and Piaget*]. Seuil.

Pineau, J. (1979). *Le mouvement rythmique en français: Principes et méthodes d'analyse* [*Rhythmic Movement in French: Principles and Methods of Analysis*]. Klincksieck.

Plato. (1997). Republic: laws; timaeus. In *Plato: Complete Works*, ed. by J. M. Cooper, & D. S. Hutchinson. Hackett Publishing Co.

Poirel, C. (1974). *Les rythmes circadiens en psychopathologie* [*Circadian Rhythms in Psychopathology*]. Masson.

Pottier, B. (1987). *Théorie et analyse en linguistique* [*Theory and Analysis in Linguistics*]. Hachette.

Prigogine, I., & Stengers, I. (1978). *La nouvelle alliance* [*The New Alliance*]. Gallimard.

Prigogine, I. (1988). *Temps et devenir: A partir de l'œuvre d'Ilya Prigogine* [*Time and Becoming: From the Work of Ilya Prigogine*]. Patino ed.

Protée. (1990). *Rythmes* [*Rhythms*], Vol. 18, no. 1. Québec.

Pratten, R. (2011). *Getting Started in Transmedia Storytelling*. Wordpress.

Rastier, F. (1987). *Sémantique interpretative* [*Interpretive Semantics*]. PUF.

Rastier, F. (1997). *Meaning and Textuality* (Collins, F. & Perron, P., Trans.). University of Toronto. (original work published 1989)

Rastier, F. (1991). *Sémantique et recherches cognitives* [*Semantics and Cognitive Research*]. PUF.

Reicha, A. (1814). *Traité de mélodie*. Chez l'auteur.

Reinberg, A. (1977). *Des rythmes biologiques à la chronobiologie* [*From Biological Rhythms to Chronobiology*]. Gauthier-Villars.

Ricœur, P. (1990). *Time and Narrative, Volume I, II, III* (McLaughlin, K., & Pellauer, D., Trans.). University of Chicago Press. (original works published 1983–1984–1985)

Salmon, C. (2017). *Storytelling: Bewitching the Modern Mind* (Macey, D., Trans.). Verso Books. (original work published 2007).

Saunders, D. S. (1977). *An Introduction to Biological Rhythms*. Blackie.

Sauvannet, P. (1989). *Pour une morphologie du rythme* [*For a Morphology of Rhythm*]. Mémoire de D.E.A.

Segal, H. (1973). *Introduction to the Work of Melanie Klein*. The Hogarth Press Ltd.

Segre, C. (1979). *Structures and Time: Narration, Poetry, Models* (Meddemmen, J., Trans.). University of Chicago Press. (original work published 1974)

Seidel, W. (1975). *Uber Rhythmus theorien der Neuzeit* [*On Rhythm Theories of the Modern Era*]. Francke.

Servien, P. (1930). *Rythmes comme introduction physique à l'esthétique* [*Rhythms as a Physical Introduction to Aesthetics*]. PUF.

Simon, J-P., & Vernet, M. (ed.). (1983). Enonciation et cinéma [Enunciation and cinema]. *Communications*, no. 38. Seuil.

Sloboda, J. A. (1985). *The Musical Mind*. Clarendon Press.

Smith, B. (ed.). (1988). *Foundations of Gestalt Theory*. Philosophia Verlag.

Sowa, J. (1984). *Conceptual Structures*. Addison-Wesley.

Steiner, R. (1966). *Gesammelte Aufsatze zur Kultur und Zeitgeschichte* [*Collected essays on Culture and Contemporary History*]. Velga der Rudolf Steiner-Nachlasverwaltung.

Stockinger, P. (1988). *Réflexion sur les notions de représentation, connaissance et raisonnement* [*Reflections on the Notions of Representation, Knowledge and Reasoning*].

Stockinger, P. (1989). A conceptual theory of state changes. *Sémiotica*, Vol. XX–XXI. Mouton de Gruyter.

Stumpf, C. (1939–1940). *Erkenntnistheorie* [*Epistemology*]. Barth.

Sulzer, J. G. (1996). General theory of the fine arts (Christensen, T., Trans.). In *Aesthetics and the Art of Musical Composition in the German Enlightenment: Selected Writings of Johann Georg Sulzer and Heinrich Christoph Koch*, ed. by N. Baker, & T. Christensen. Cambridge University Press. (original work published 1972)

Talmy, L. (1983). How language structures space. In *Spatial Orientation: Theory, Research and Application*, ed. by H. Pick, & L. Acredolo. Plenum.

Talmy, L. (1985). *Force Dynamics in Language and Thought. Parasessions on Causatives and Agentivity*. Chicago Linguistic Society (21st Regional Meeting), University of Chicago.

Tenderich, B. (2014). *Transmedia Branding*. DE: EMIO.

Thom, R. (1973). De l'icône au symbole: Esquisse d'une théorie générale du symbolism [From con to symbol: outline of a general theory of symbolism]. *Les cahiers internationaux du symbolism*, no. 22–23.

Thom, R. (1990). La danse comme sémiurgie [Danse as semiurgy]. *Apologie du logos*, Hachette.

Thom, R. (1990). *Semio Physics: A Sketch* (Meyer, V., Trans.). Addison-Wesley Publishing Company. (original work published 1988)

Thom, R. (1991). *Apologie du logos* [*Apology of logos*]. Hachette.

Todorov, T. (1981). *Mikhail Bakhtin. Le principe dialogique*. SEUIL.

Valery, P. (2000). *Cahiers/Notebooks* (Killick, R., Trans.). Peter Lang Pub. Inc. (original work published 1973)

Varela, F. (1986). *Connaître: Les Sciences Cognitives tendences et perspectives* [*To Know: Cognitive Science Trends and Perspectives*]. Seuil.

Varela, F., Thompson, E., & Rosch, E. (1991). *The Embodied Mind*. MIT Press.

Vignaux, G. (1988). *Le discours acteur du monde* [*The World's Actor Discourse*]. Ophrys.

Vincent d'Indy, V. (1903). *Musical composition*.

Volli, U. (1991). *Apologia del silenzio imperfetto* [*Apology of Imperfect Silence*]. Feltrinelli.

Weinrich, H. (1964). *Tempus* (Brown, J. K., & Brown, M., Trans.). Fordham University Press.

Wertheimer, M. (1938). Numbers and numerical concepts in primitive people. In *A Source Book of Gestalt Psychology*, ed. by W. D. Ellis. Kegan Paul, Trench, Trubner & Company. (pp. 265–273). https://doi.org/10.1037/11496-022

Wertheimer, M. (1912). Experimentelle Studien über das Sehen von Bewegung. *Zeitschrift für Psychologie*, 61(1), 161–265.

Wertheimer, M. (1923). Untersuchüngen zu Lehre von des Gestalt [Investigations into the Doctrine of Gestalt]. In *Principles of Perceptual Organization*, ed. by W. R. Beardslee, & M. Wertheimer. (pp. 301–350).

Wertheimer, M. (1938). Laws of organization in perceptual forms. In *A Source Book of Gestalt Psychology*, ed. by W. D. Ellis. Routledge & Keagan. (pp. 71–88).

Willems, E. (1954). *Le rythme musical-métrique*. PUF.

Winfree, A. T. (1974). Rotating chemical reactions. *Scientific American*, no. 230. (pp. 82–95).

Wunenburger, J. J. (ed.). (1992). *Les rythmes* [*Rhythms*]. L'Harmattan.

Zeeman, E. C. (1972). Differential equations for the heartbeat and nerve impulse. In *Towards a Theoretical Biology*, ed. by C. H. Waddington. Edinburgh University Press. (pp. 8–67).

Zilberberg, C. (1985). *Information rythmique* [*Rhythmic Information*]. Phoriques.

Zilberberg, C. (1988). Actualité de Brøndal [News from Brøndal]. *Raison et poétique du sens*. PUF.

Zilberberg, C. (1989a). Le rythme revisité. *Cahiers de sémiotique textuelle*. Université Paris X.

Zilberberg, C. (1989b). Modalité et pensée modale [Modality and modal thinking]. *Nouveaux Actes Sémiotiques*. PULIM.

Zilberberg, C. (1992). Présence de Wölfflin [Presence of Wölfflin]. *Nouveaux Actes Sémiotiques*. PULIM.

Zinna, A. (1992). Un soggetto per l'estesia [A subject for esthesia]. *Semio-News*. Università di Bologna.

Zinna, A. (1993). Teorie narrative e stilistica [Narrative theories and stylistics]. *Semio-News*. Università di Bologna.

Printed and bound by CPI Group (UK) Ltd, Croydon, CR0 4YY
23/08/2023